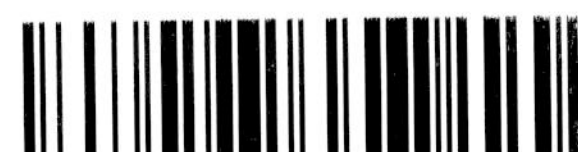

Christmas Coloring Book for Kids!

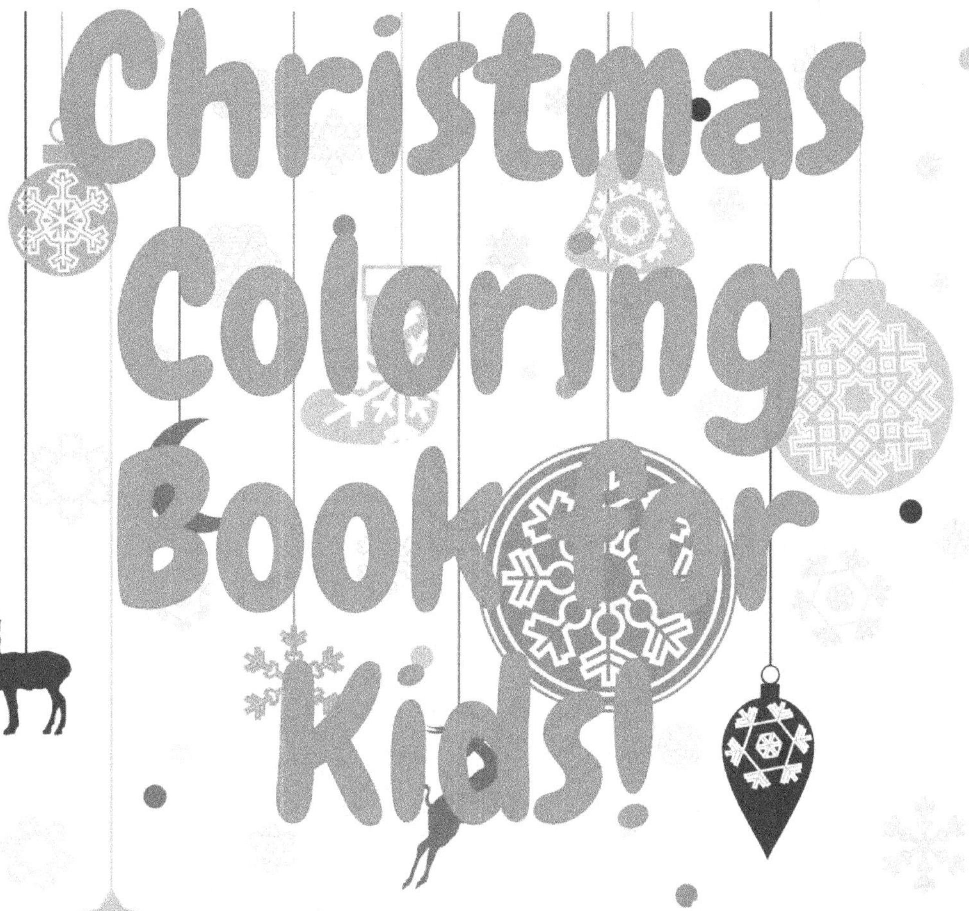

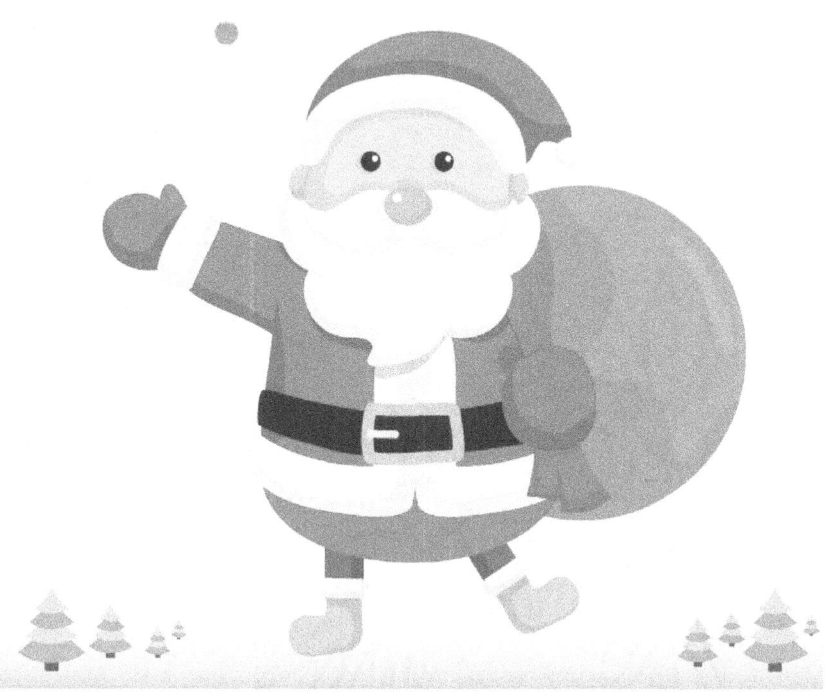

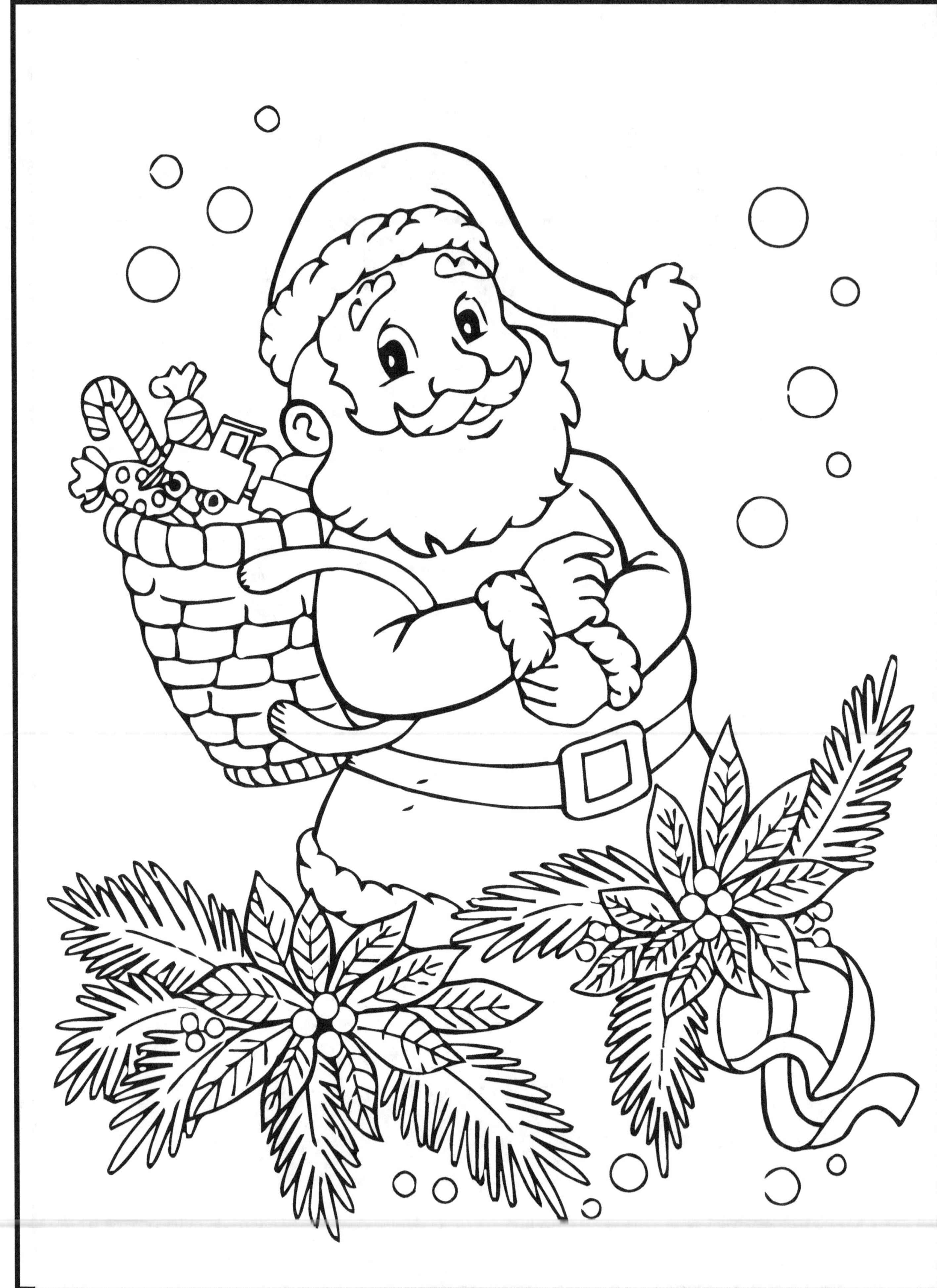

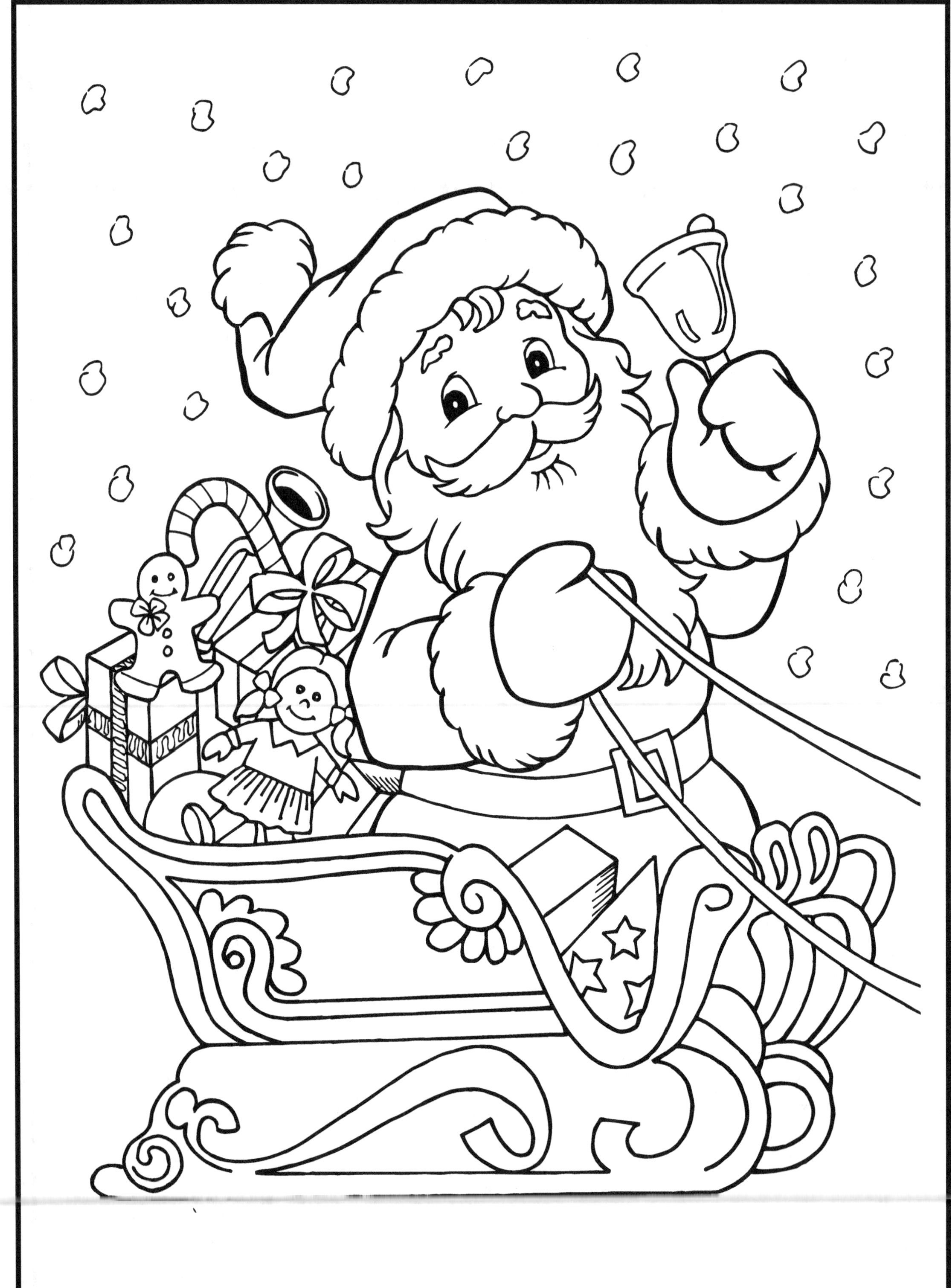

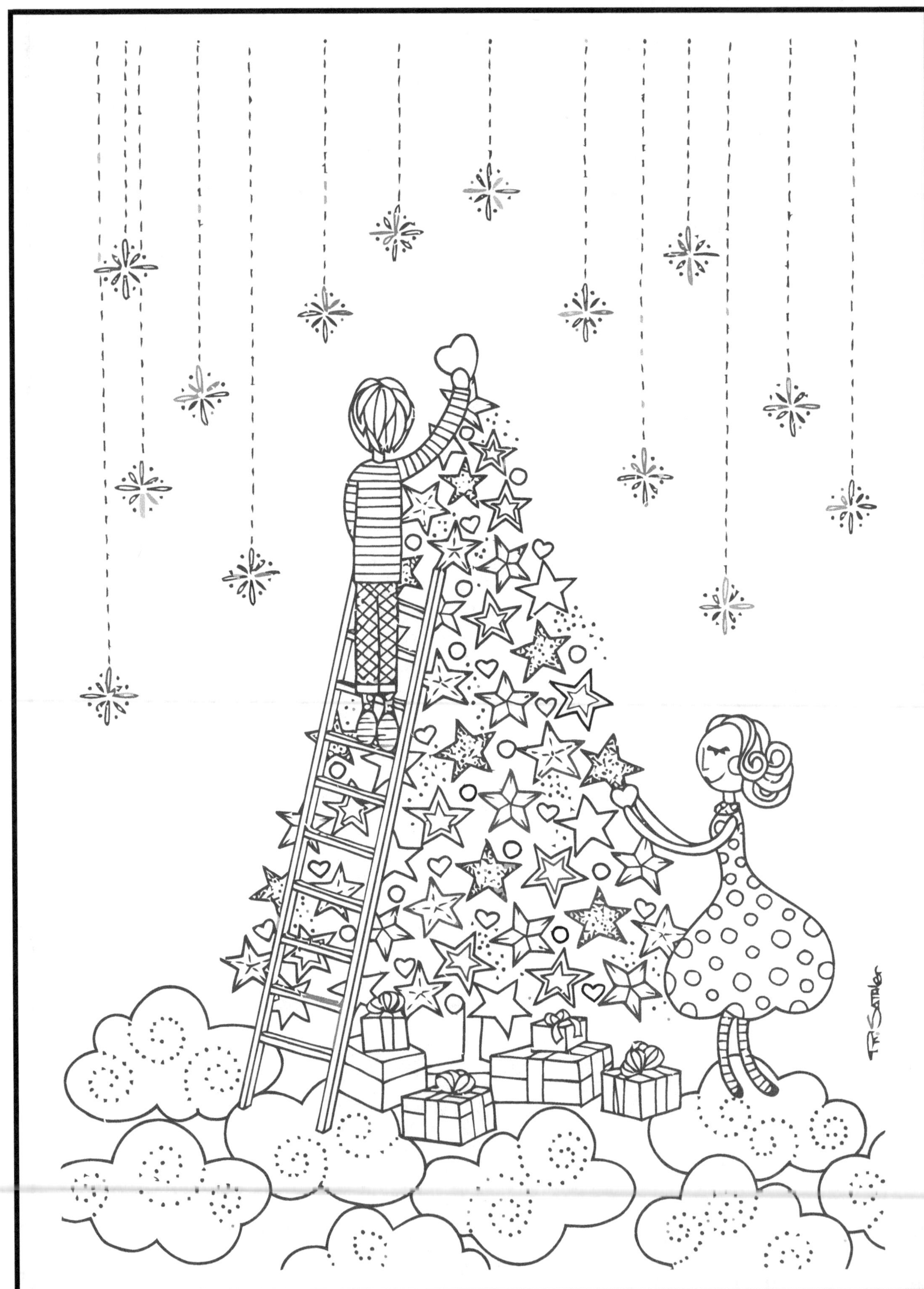

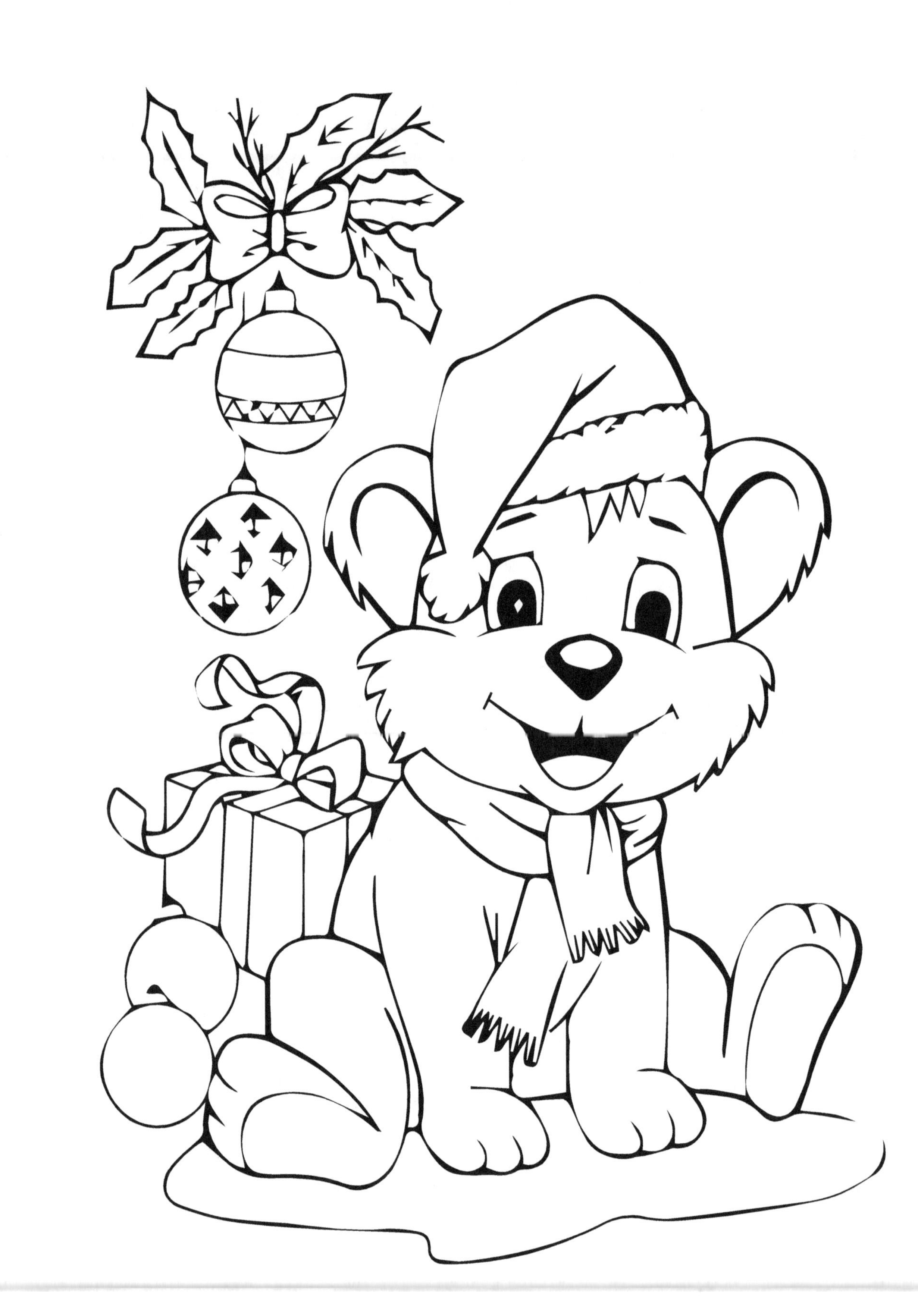

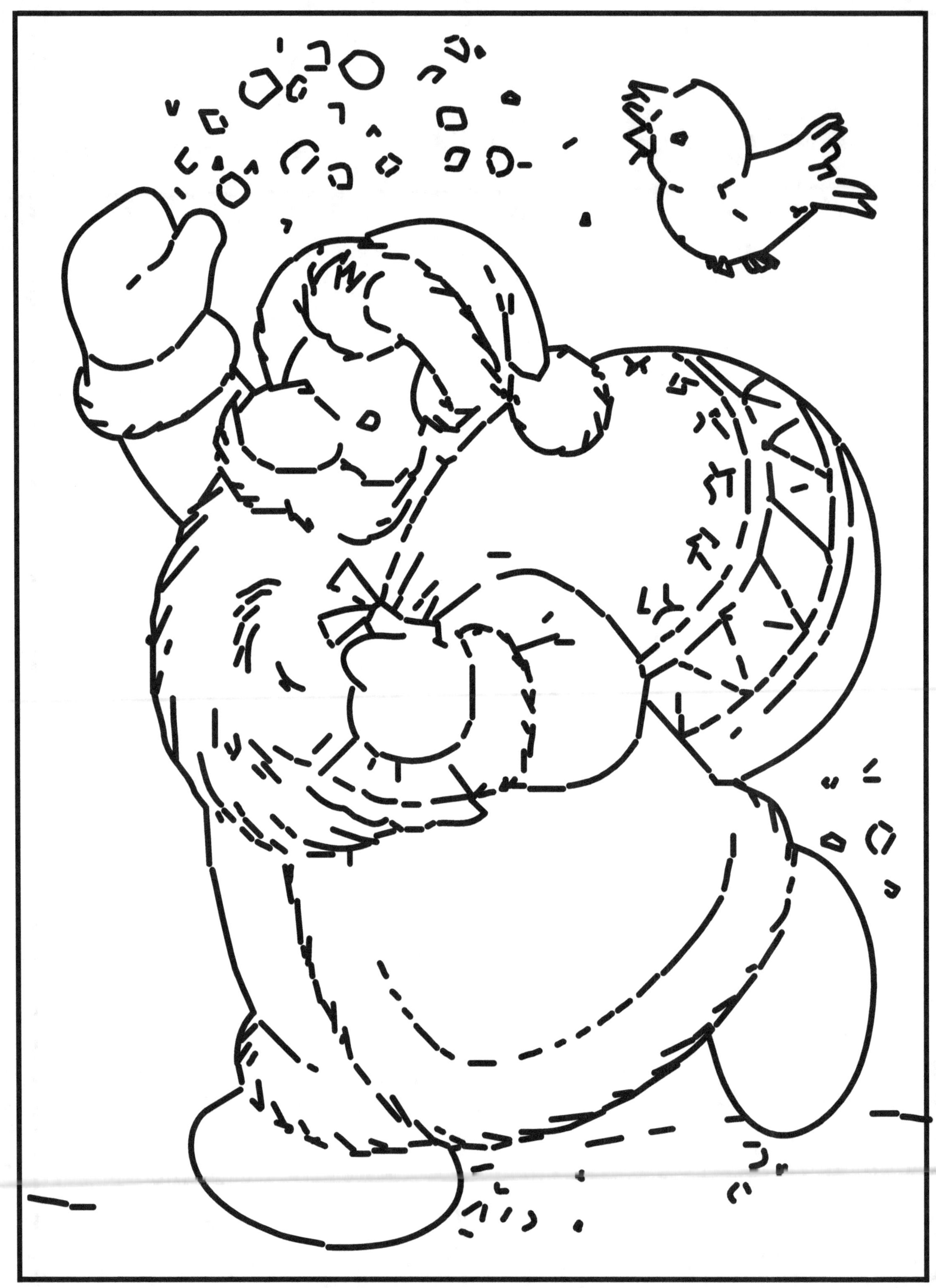

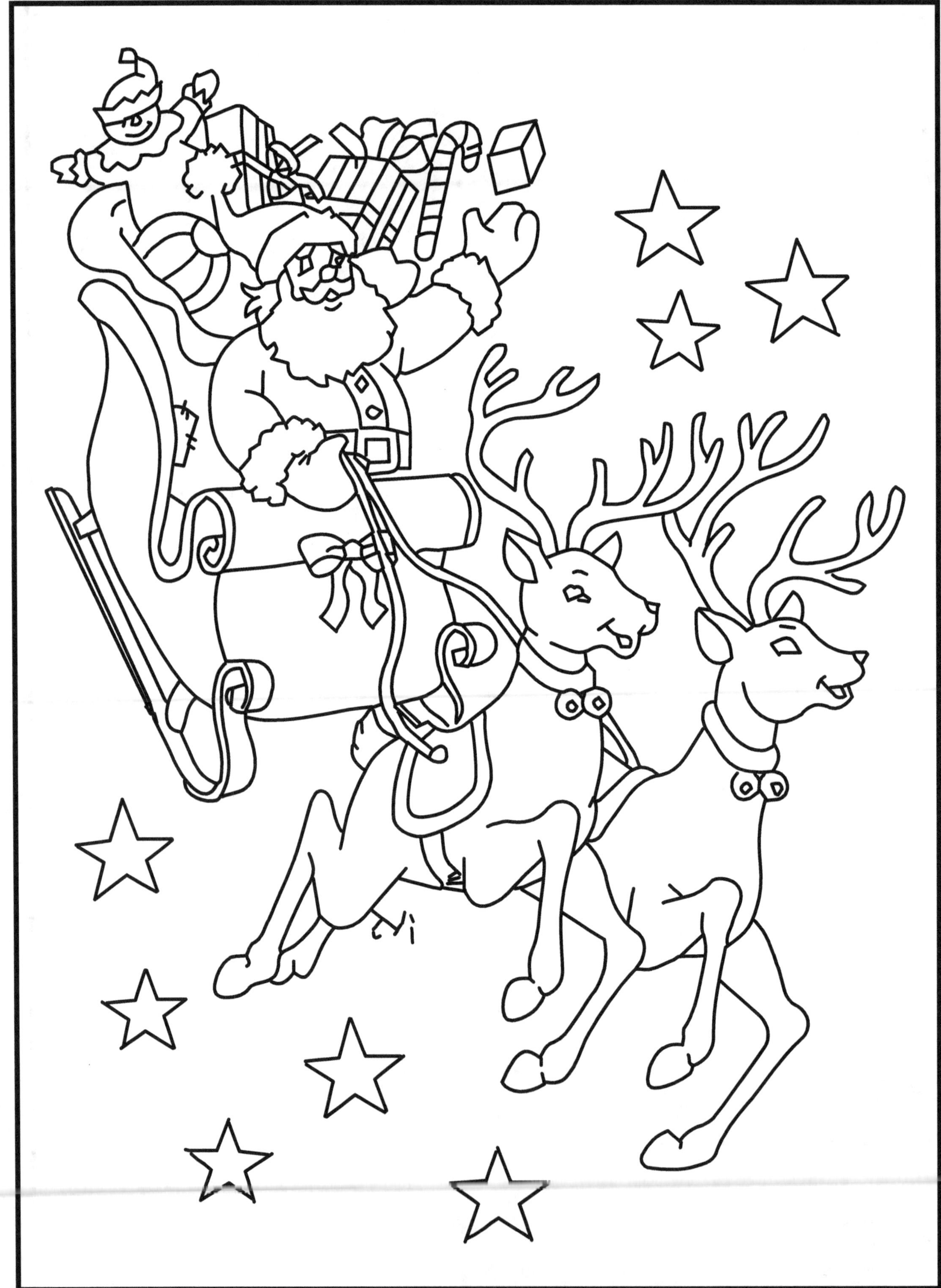

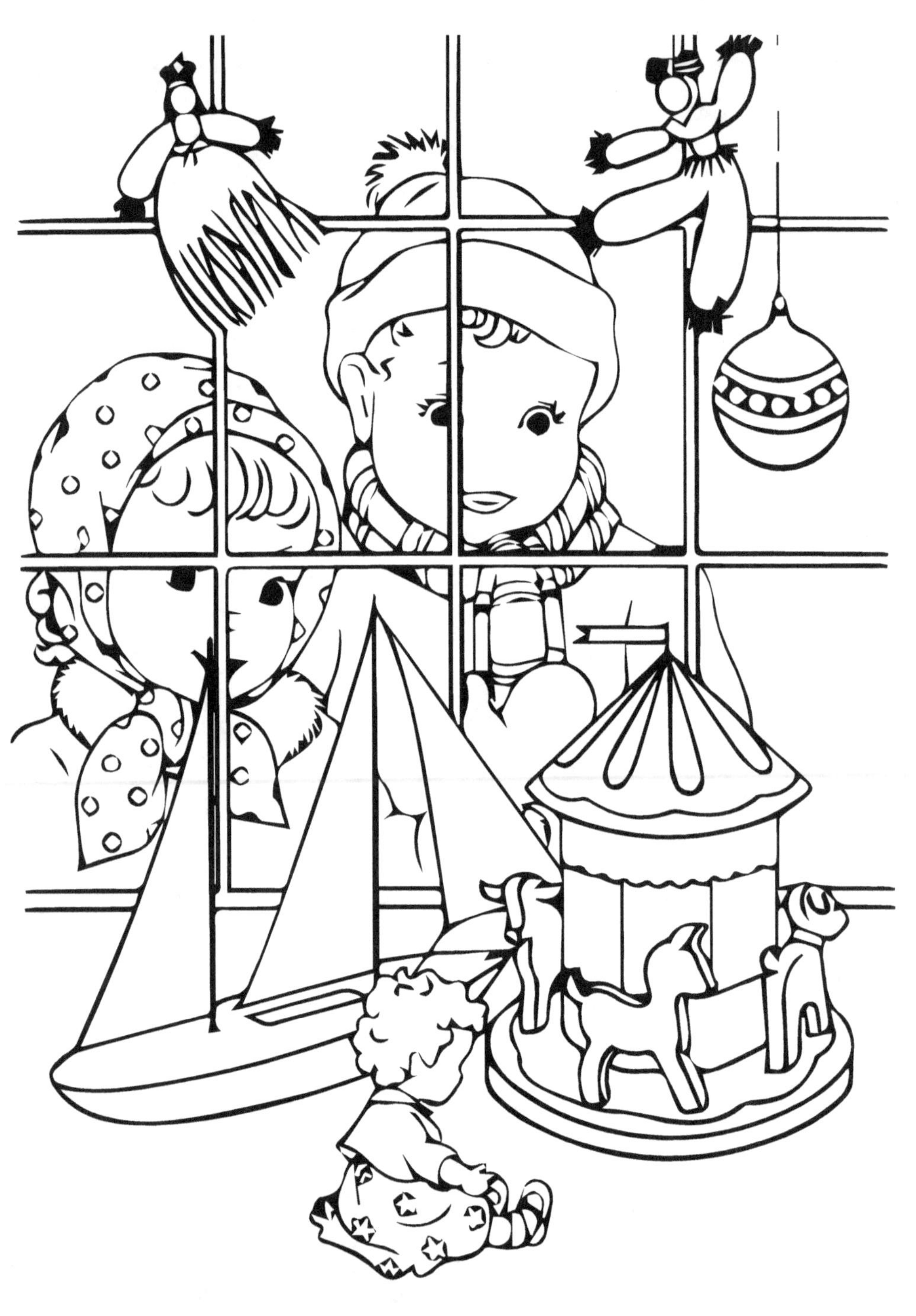

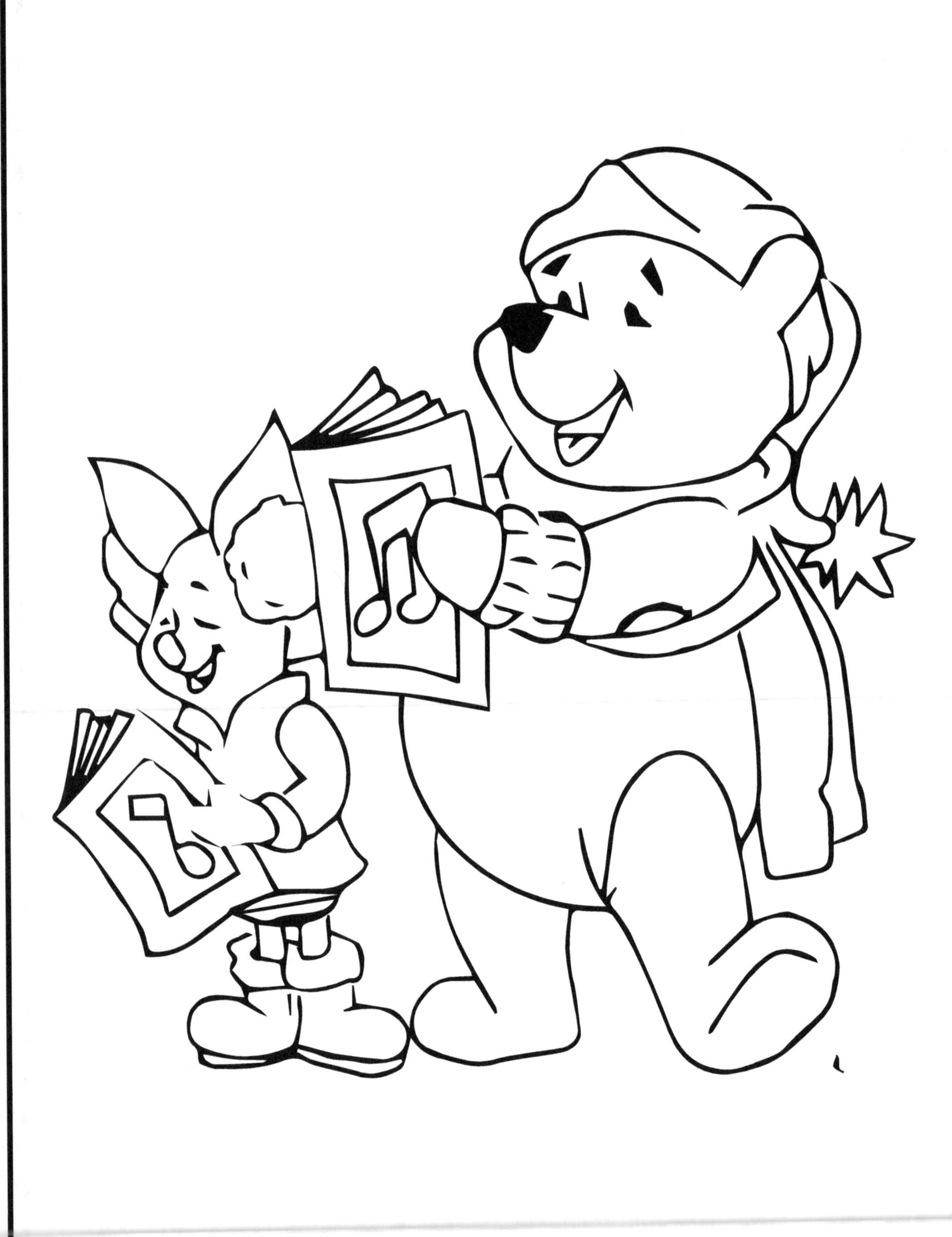

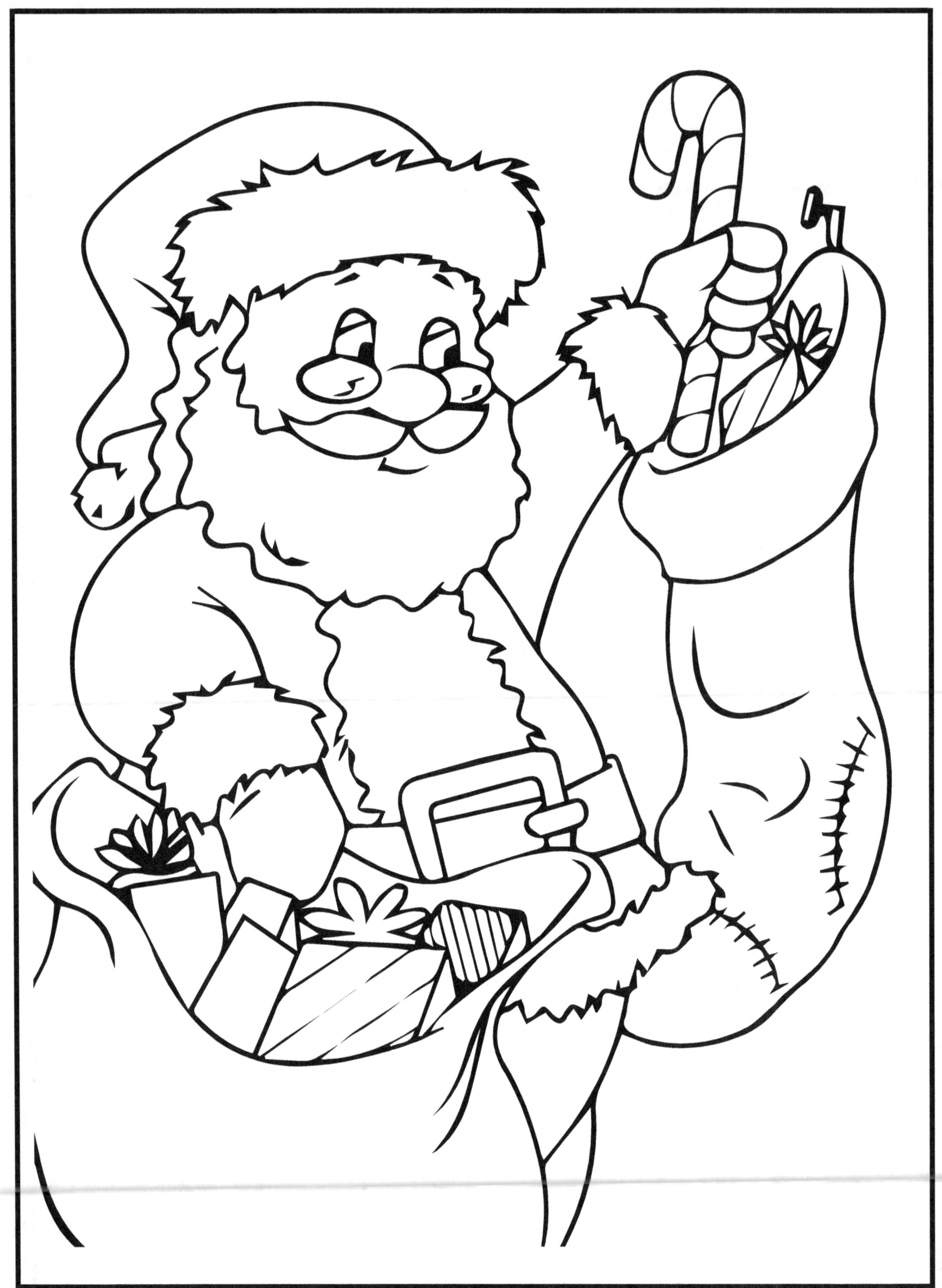

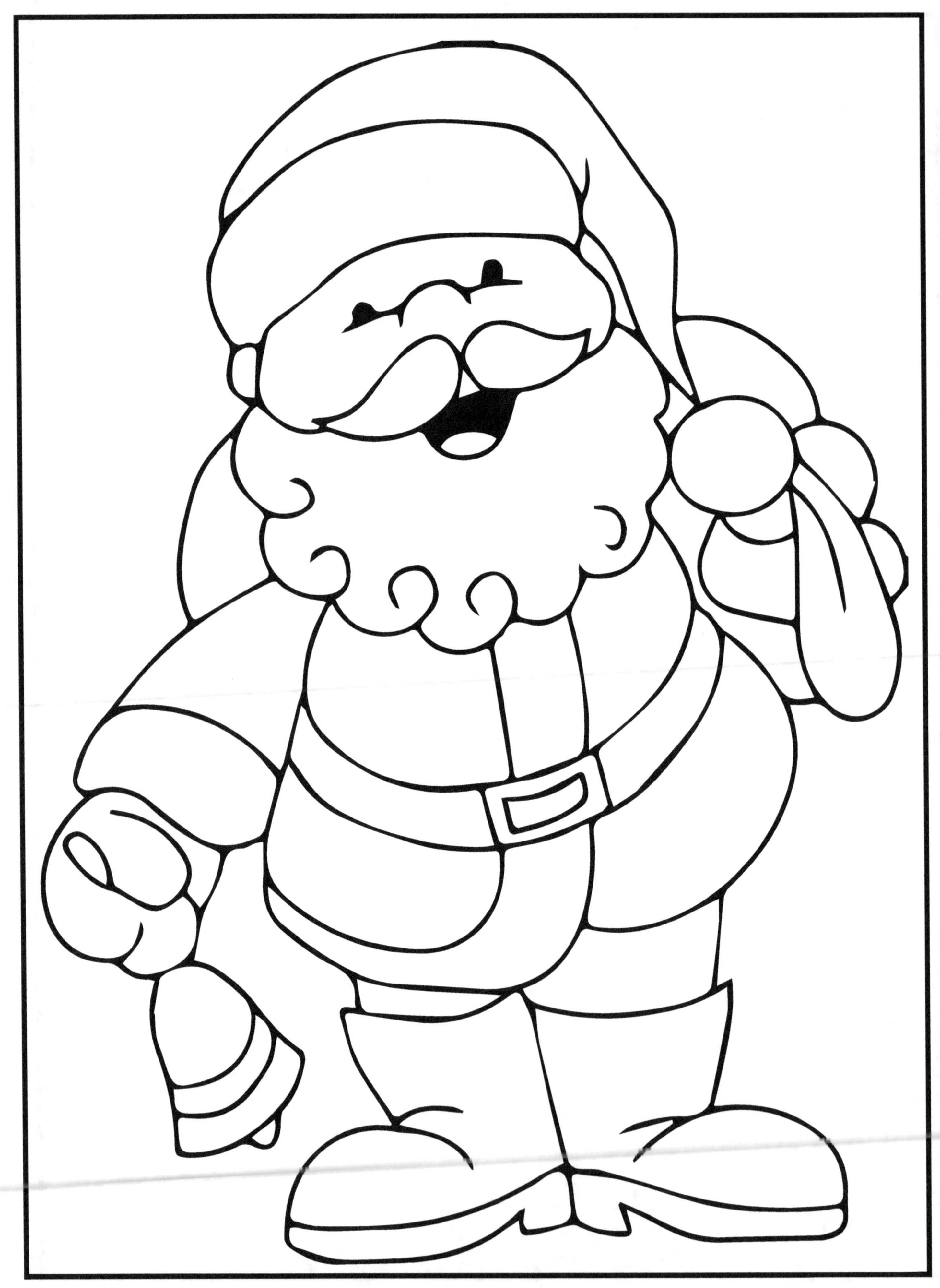

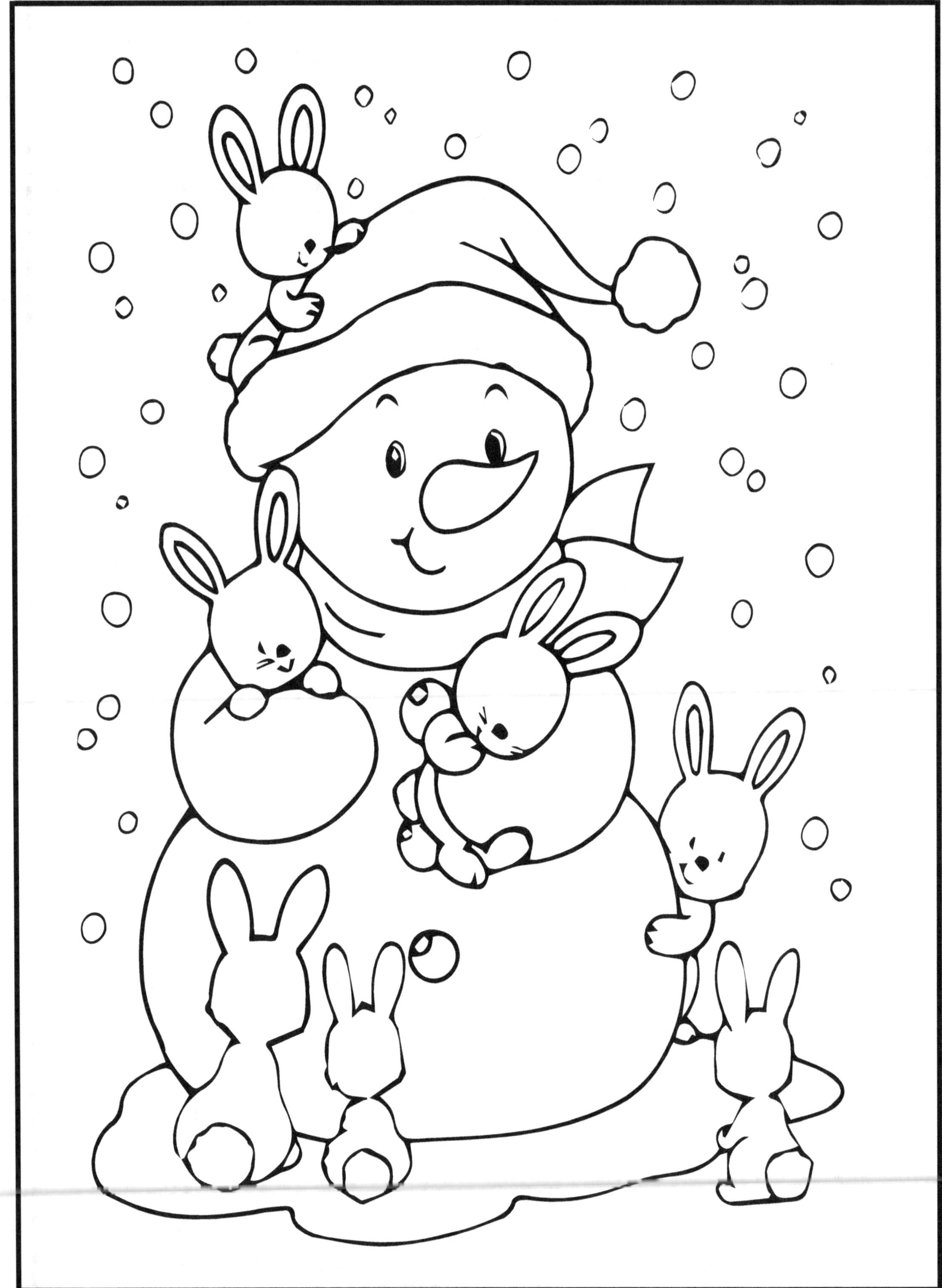

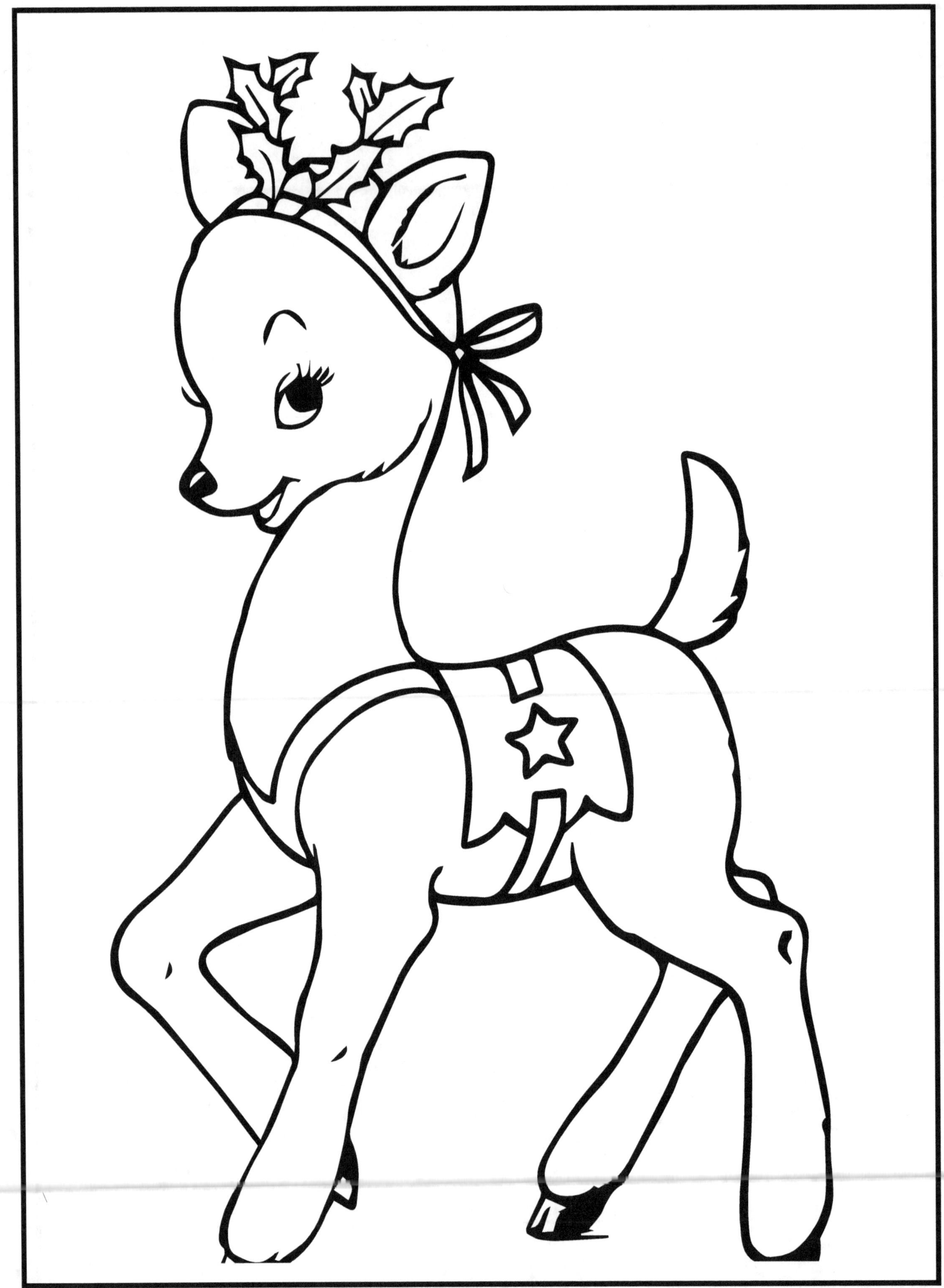

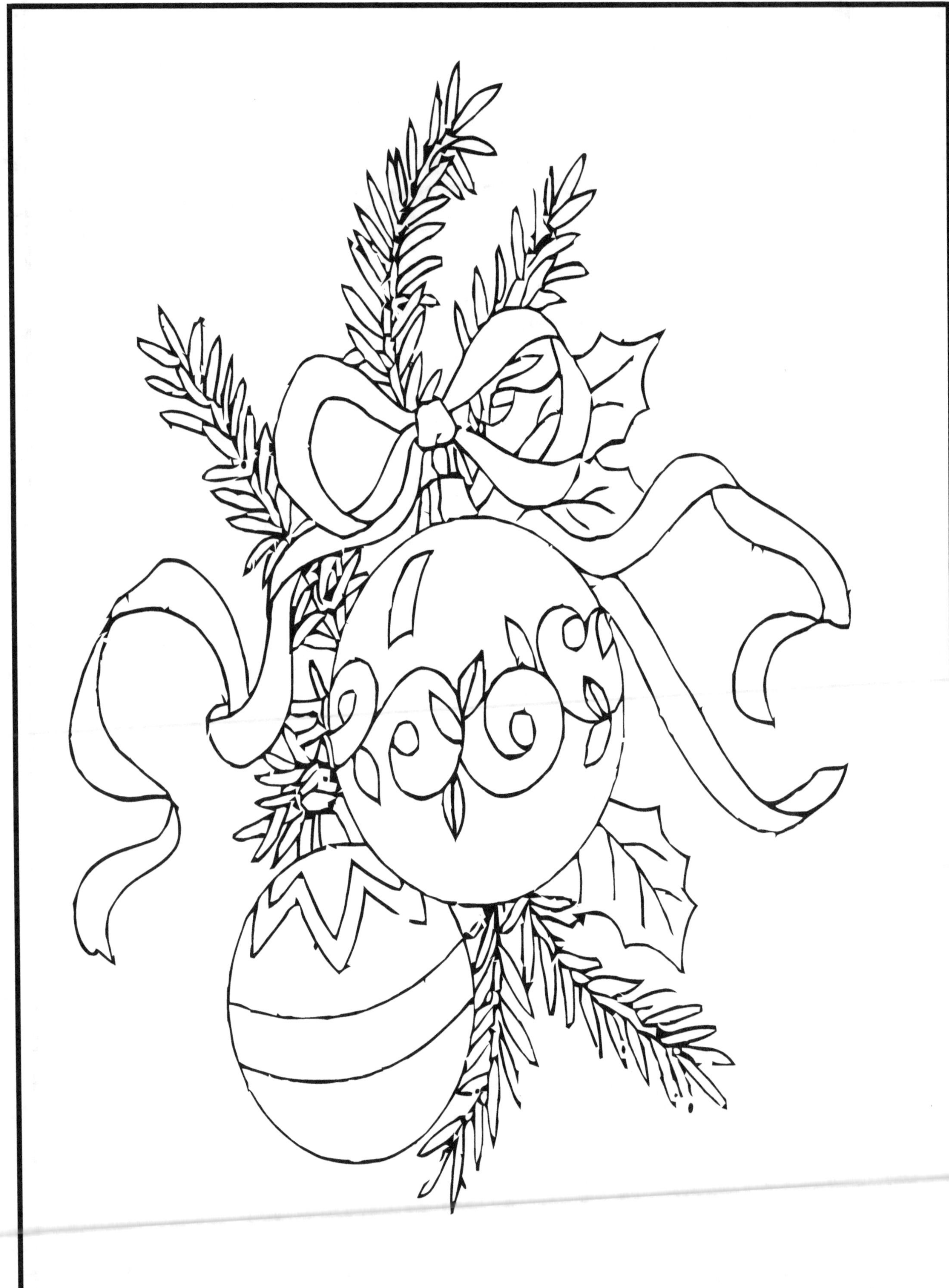

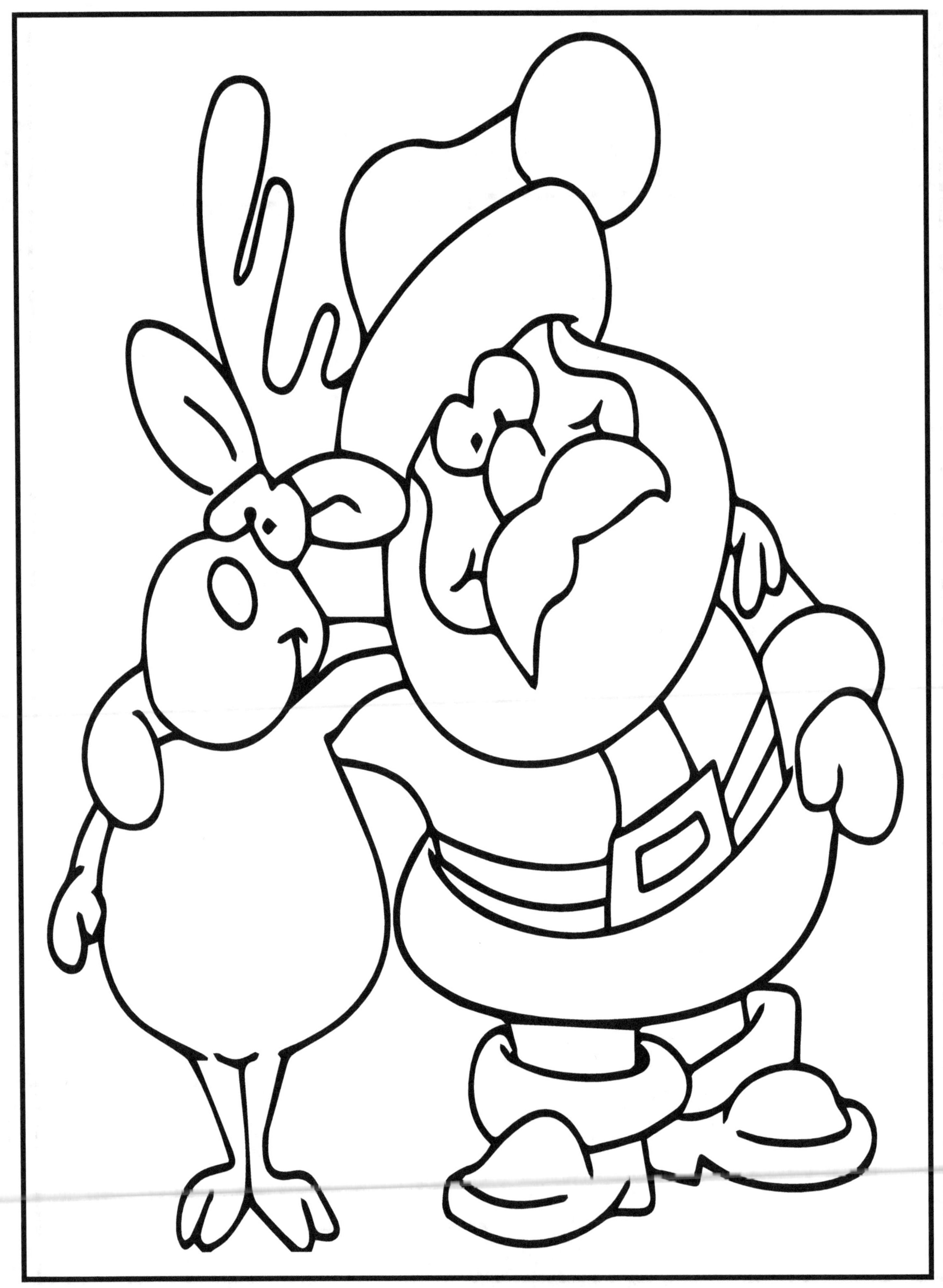

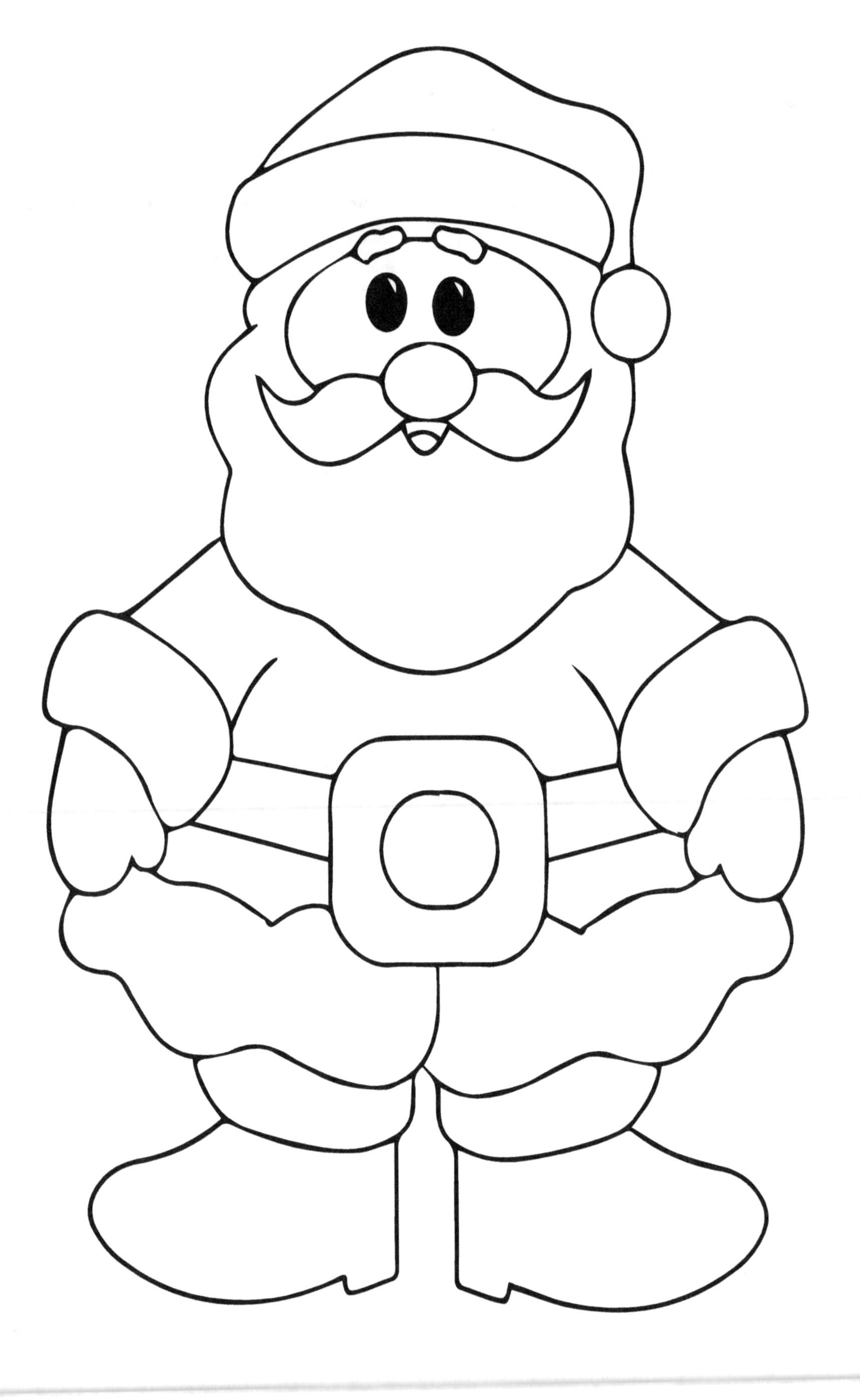

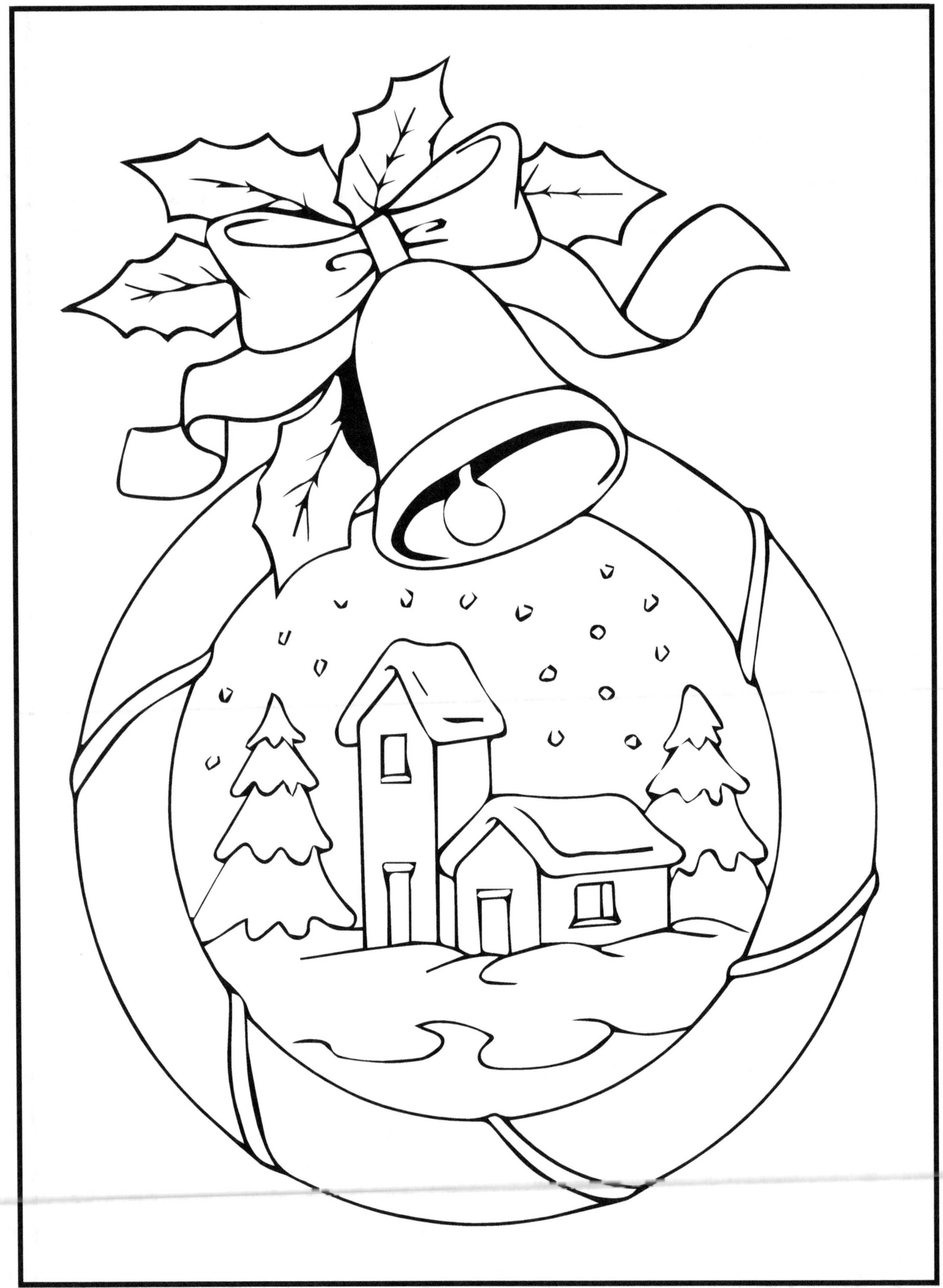

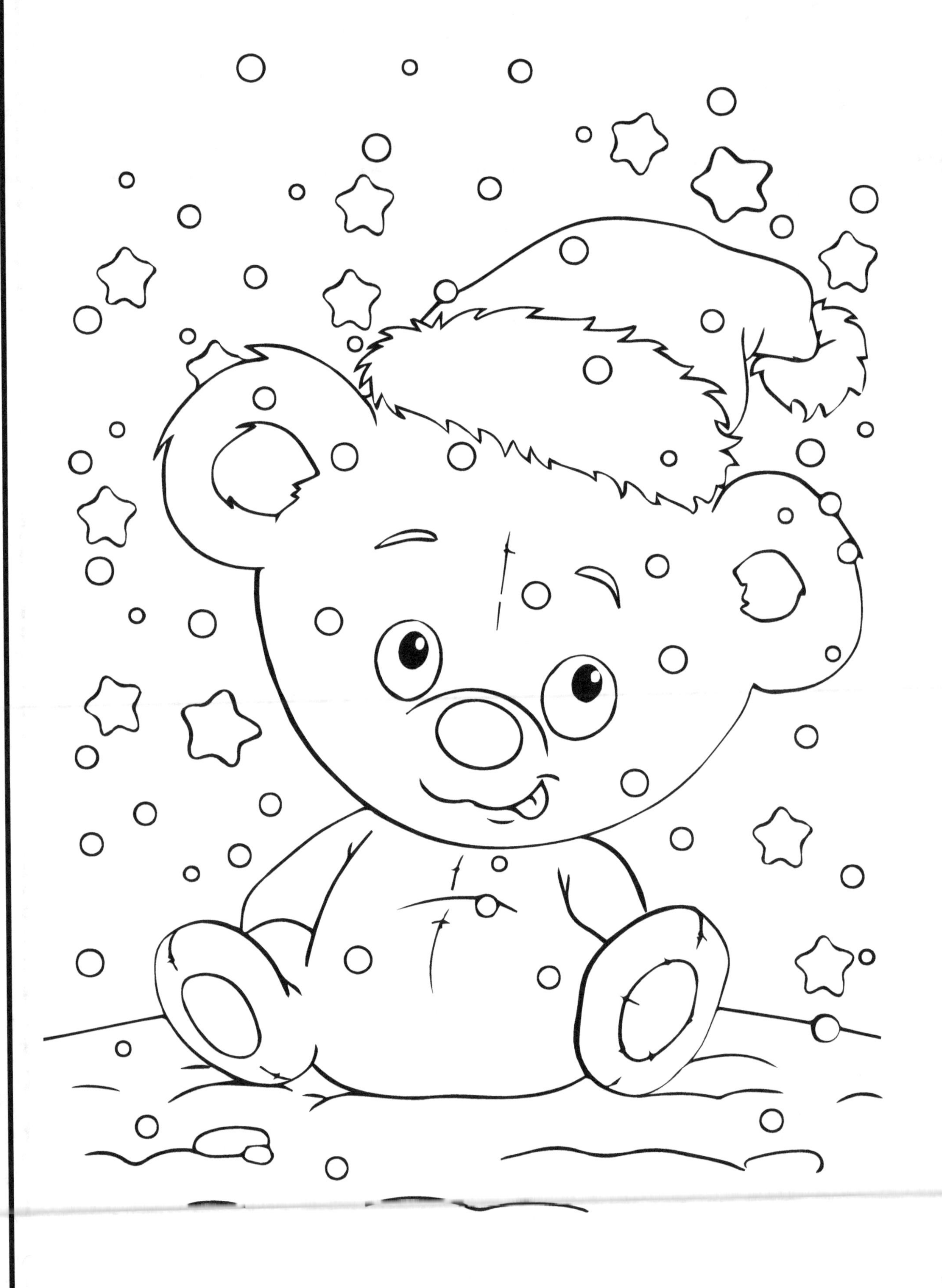

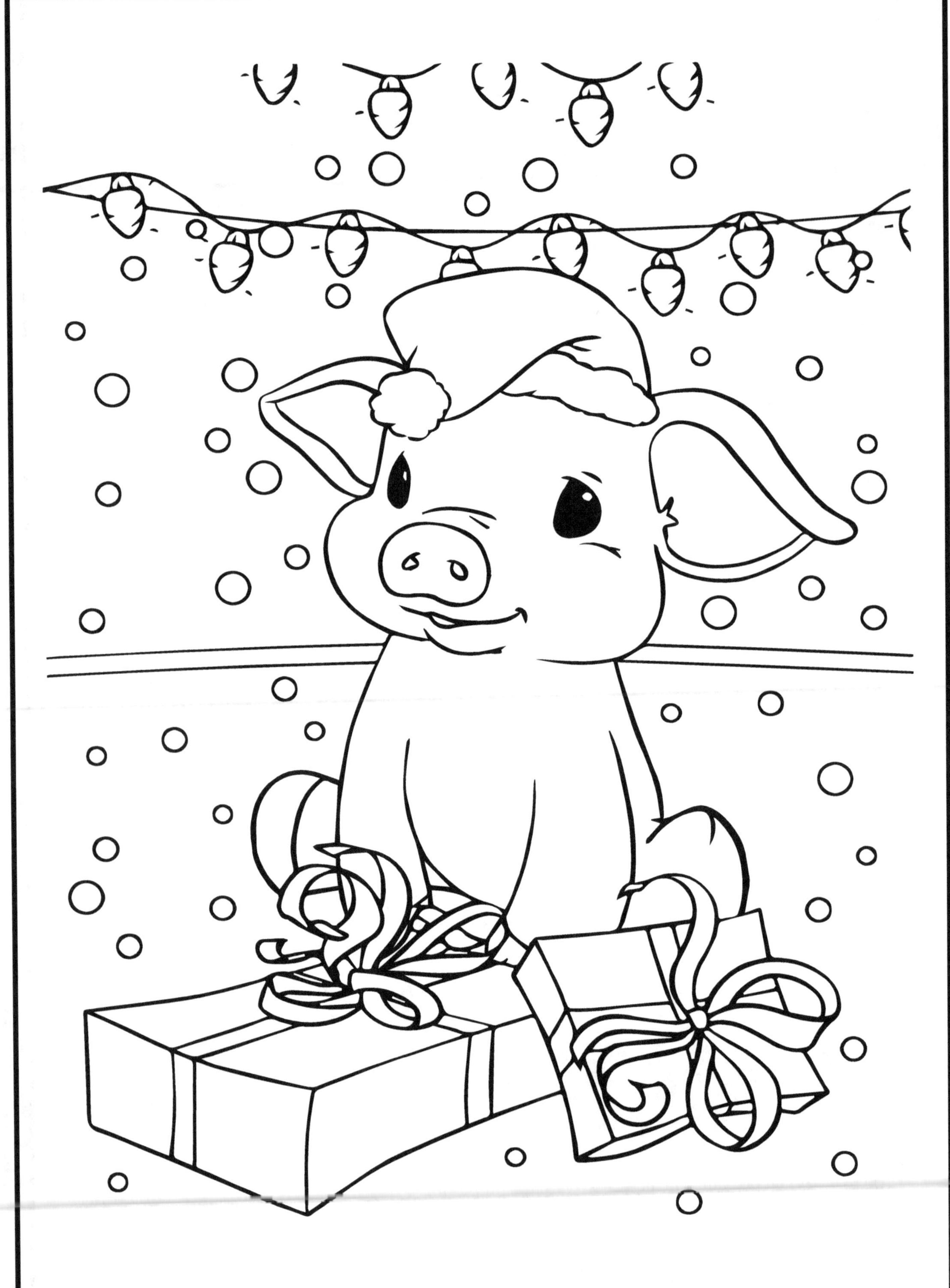

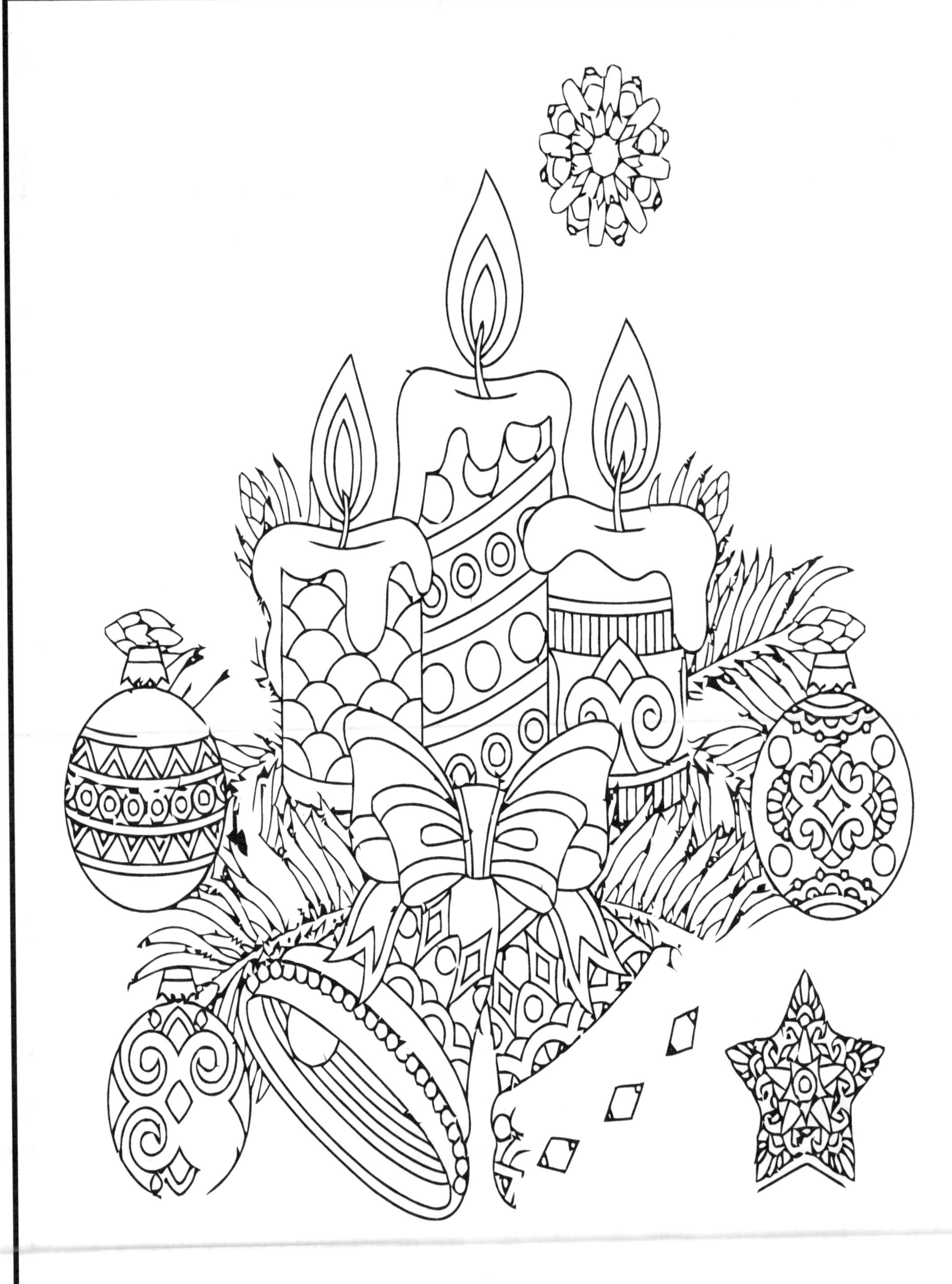

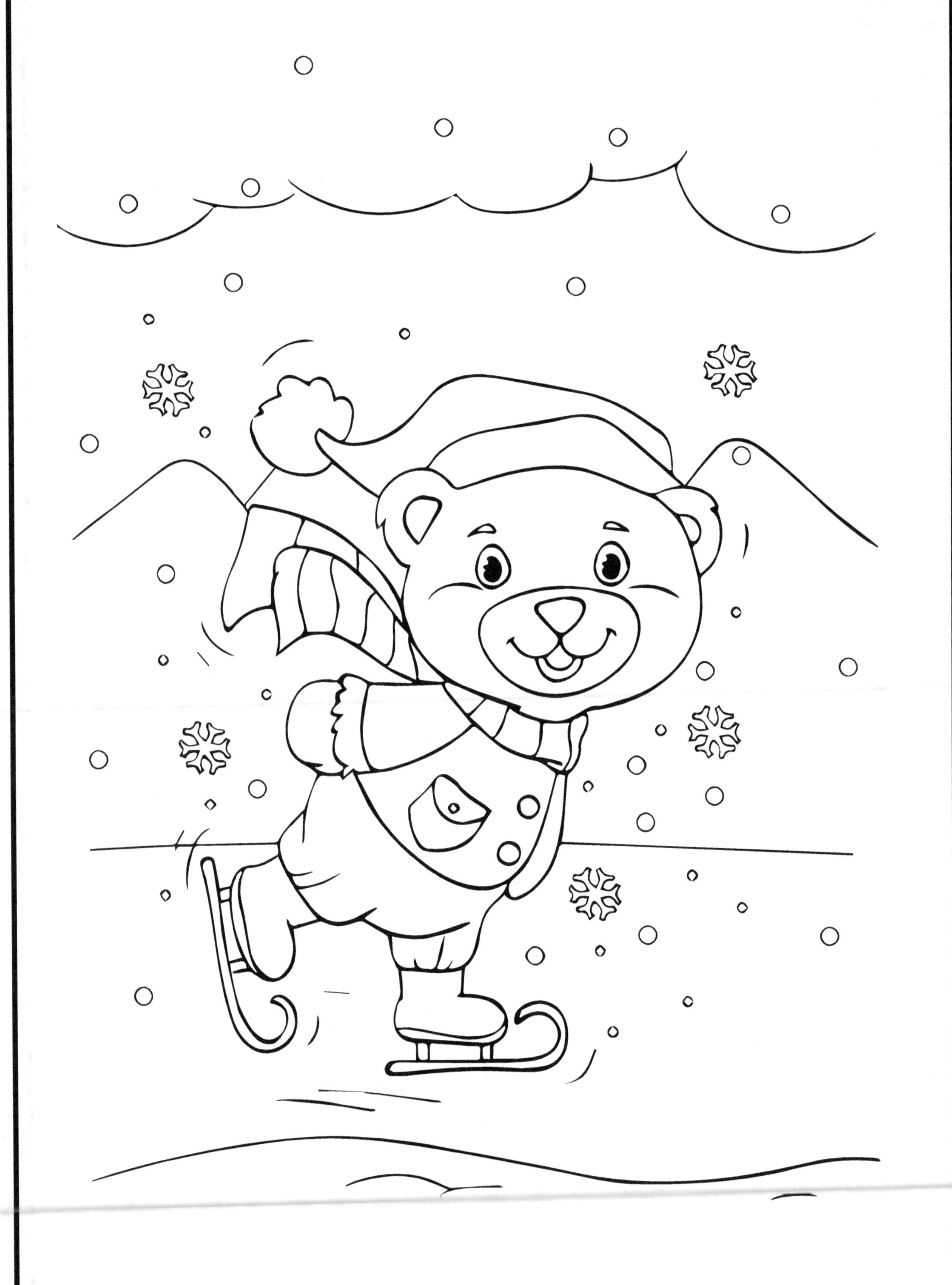

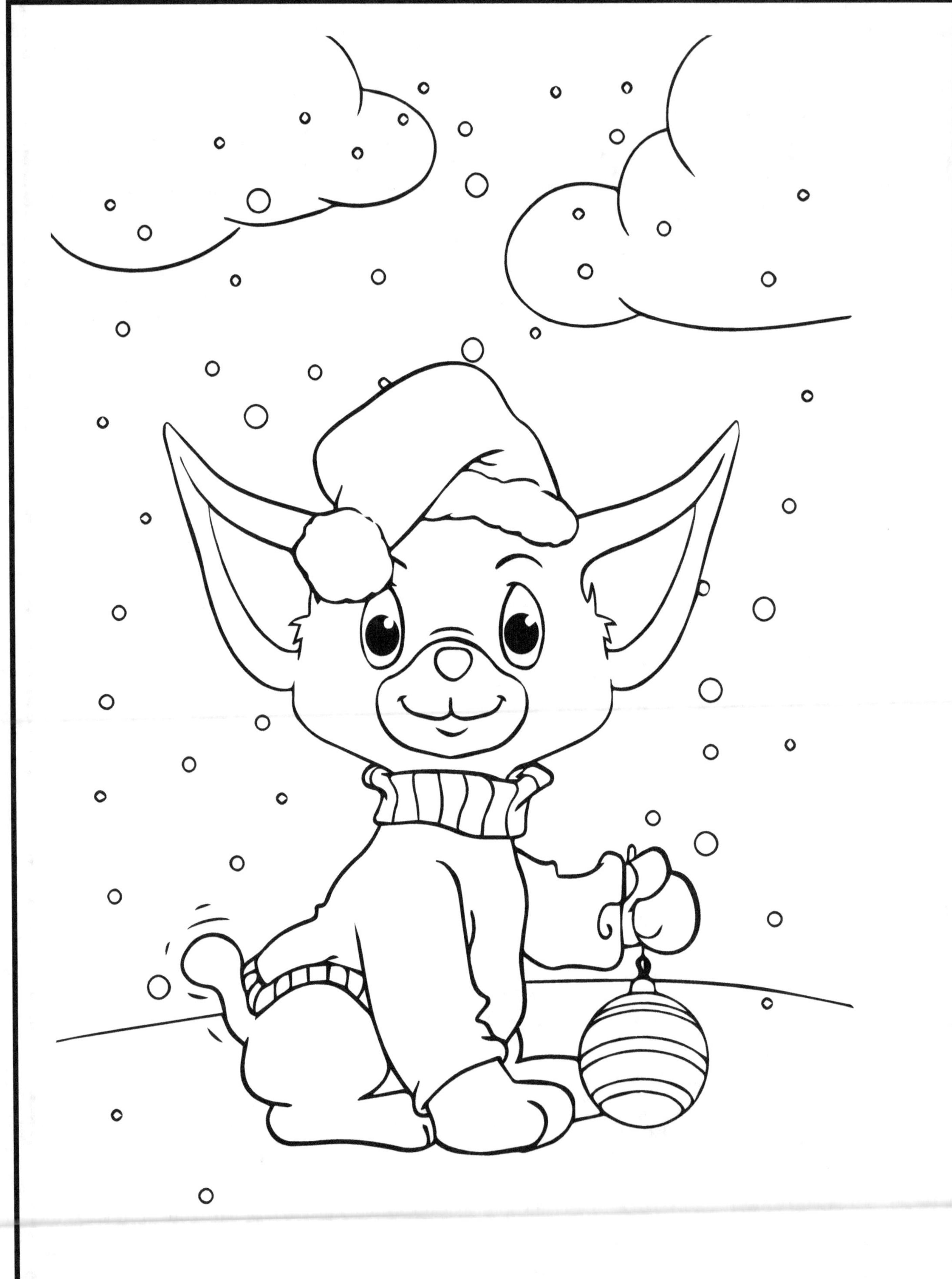

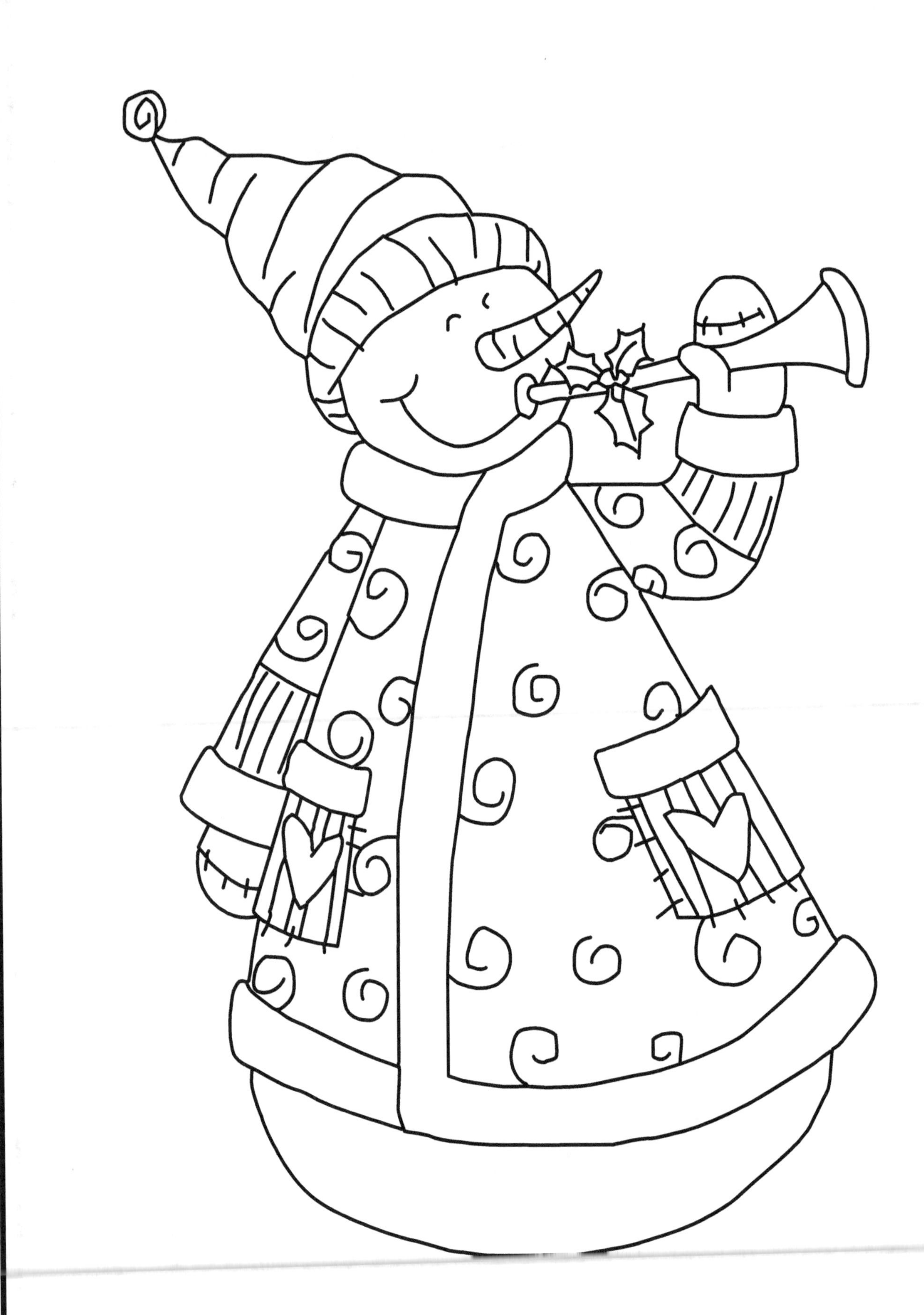

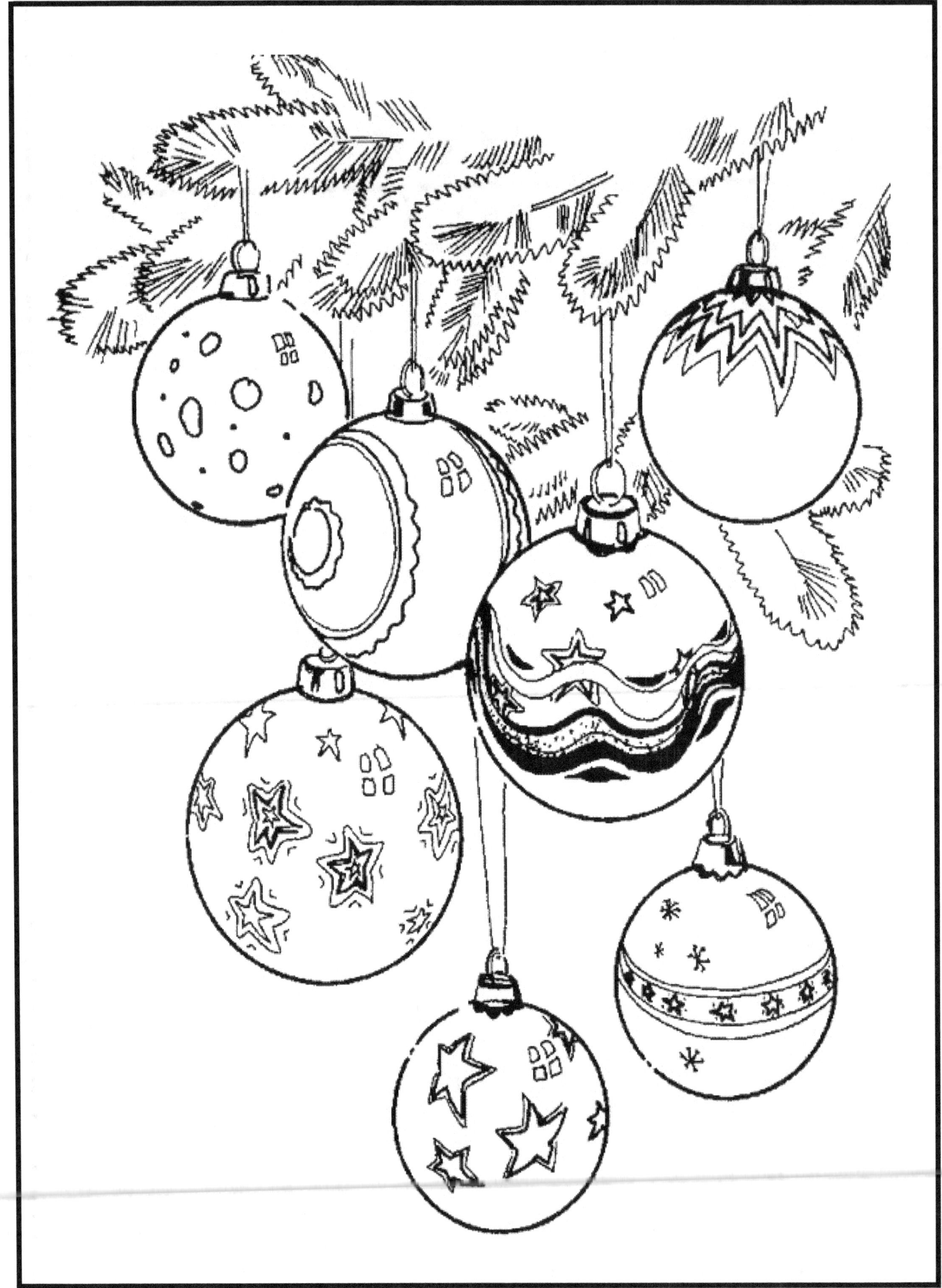

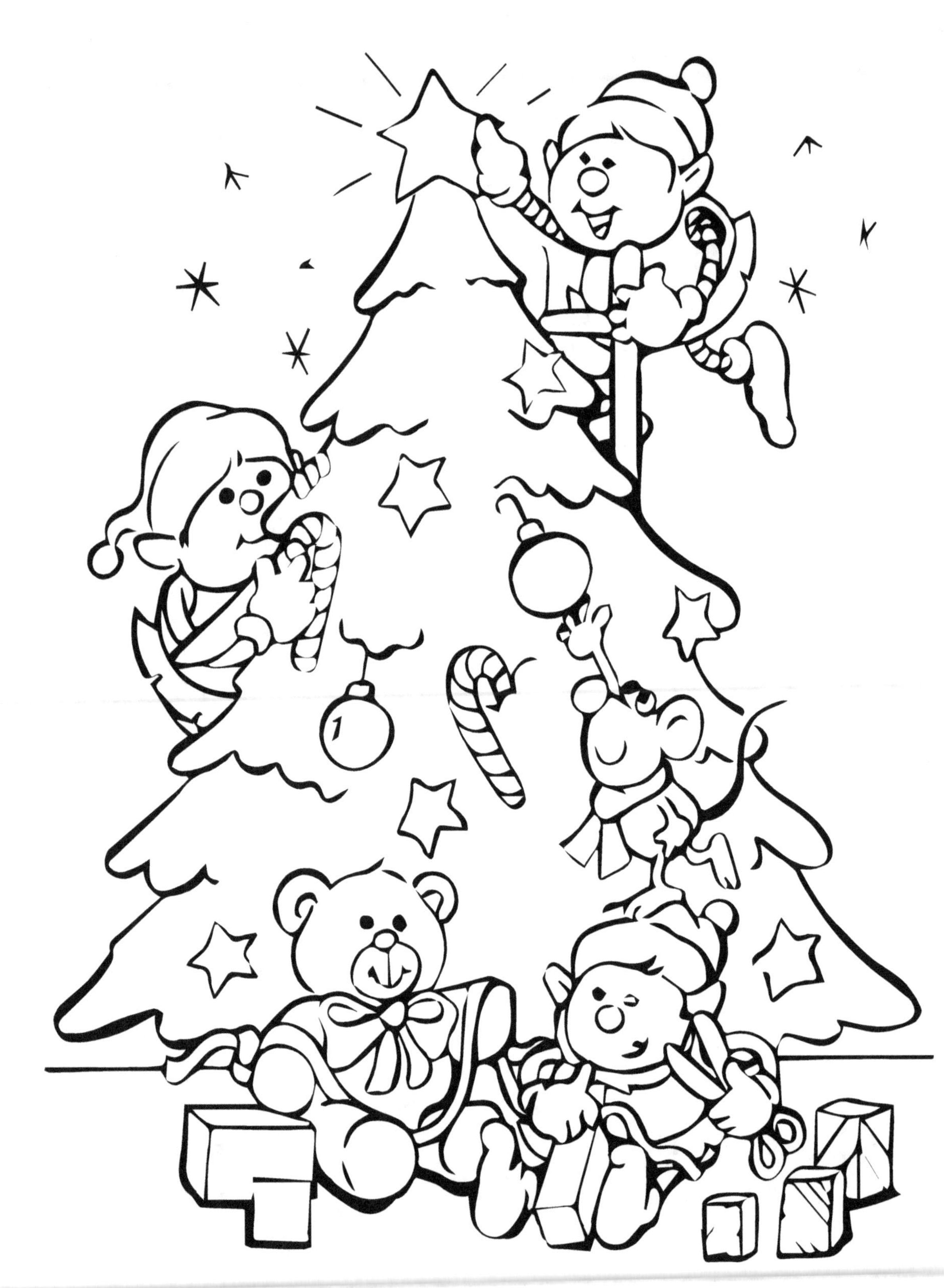

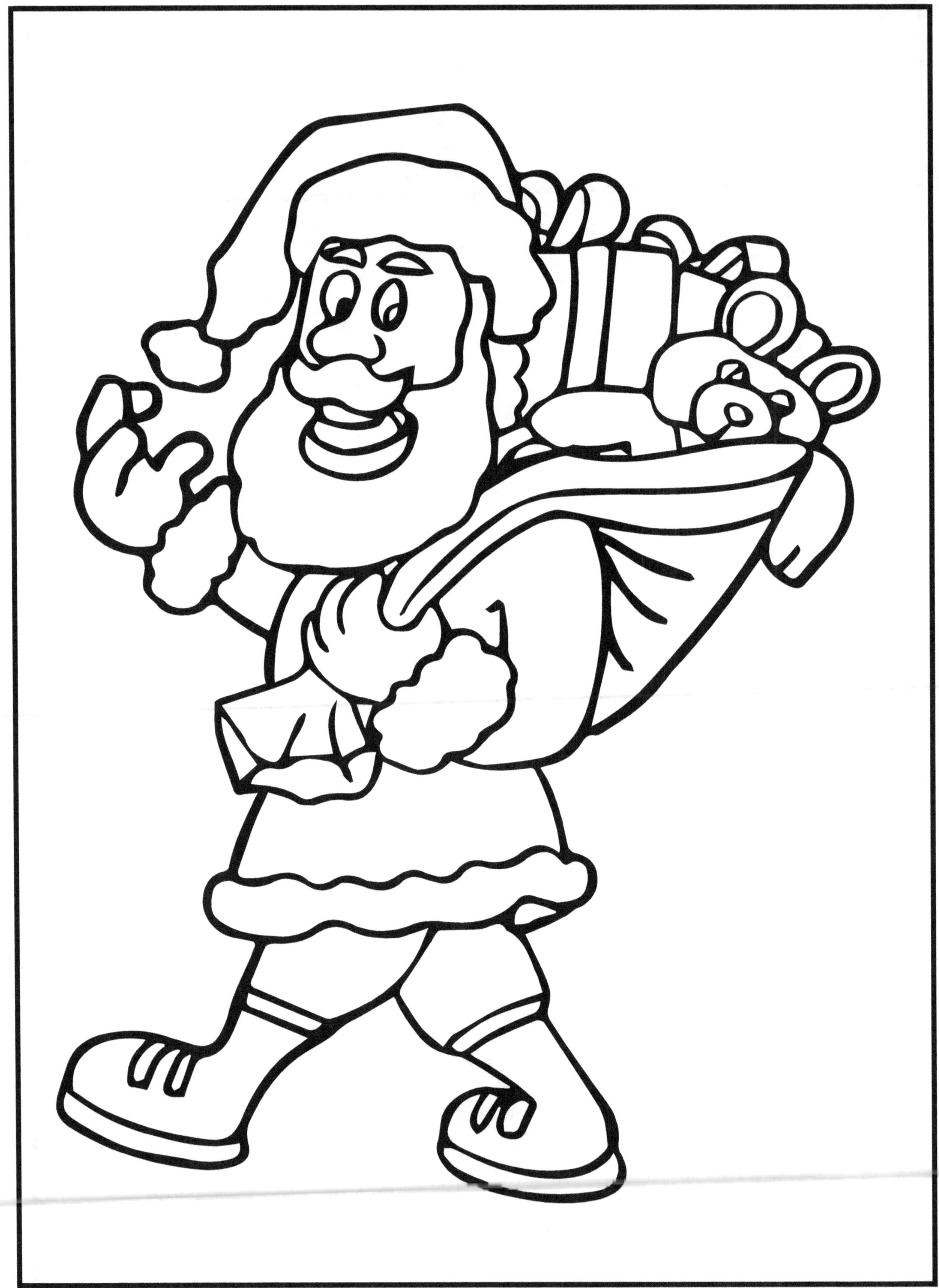

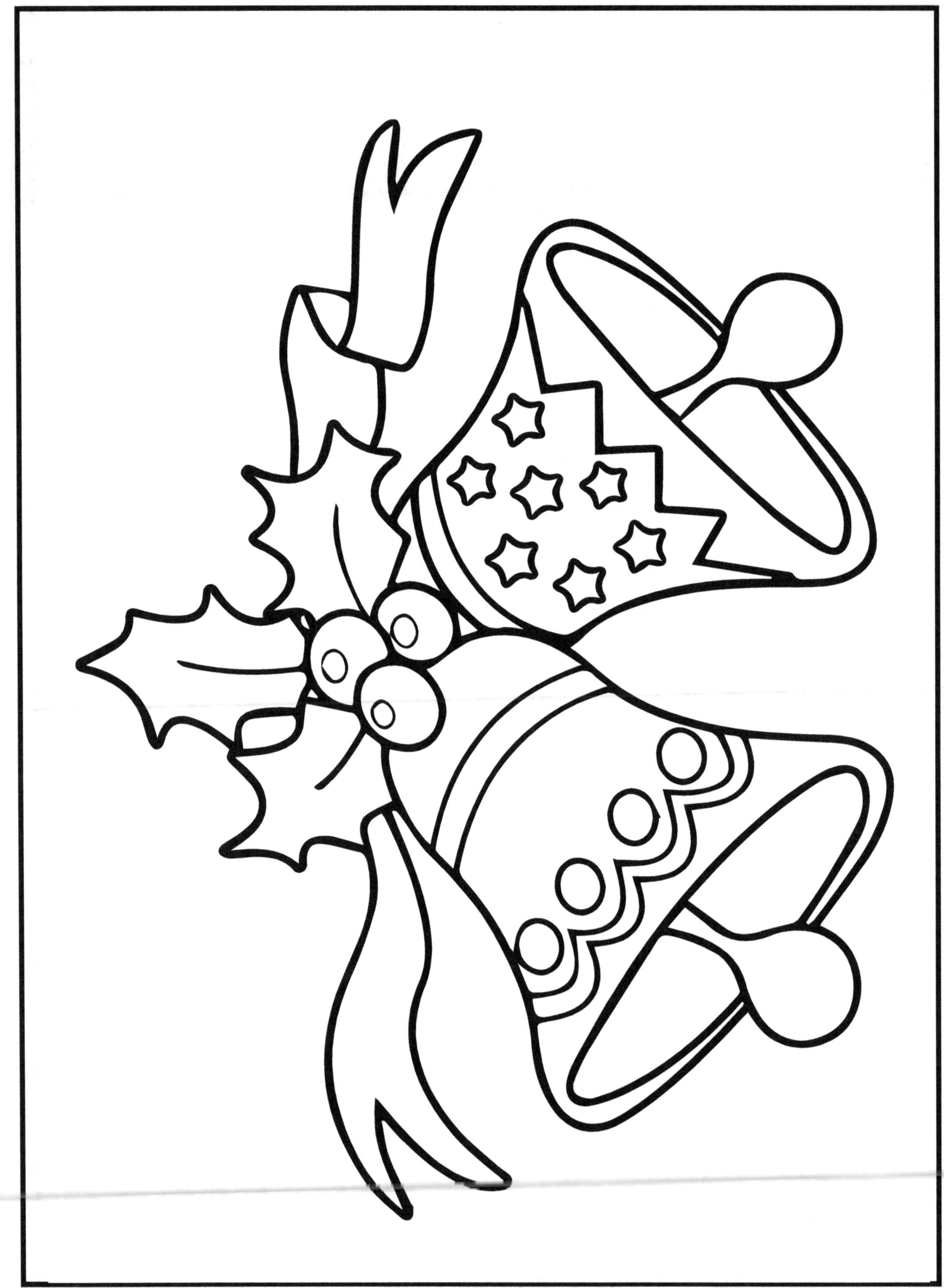

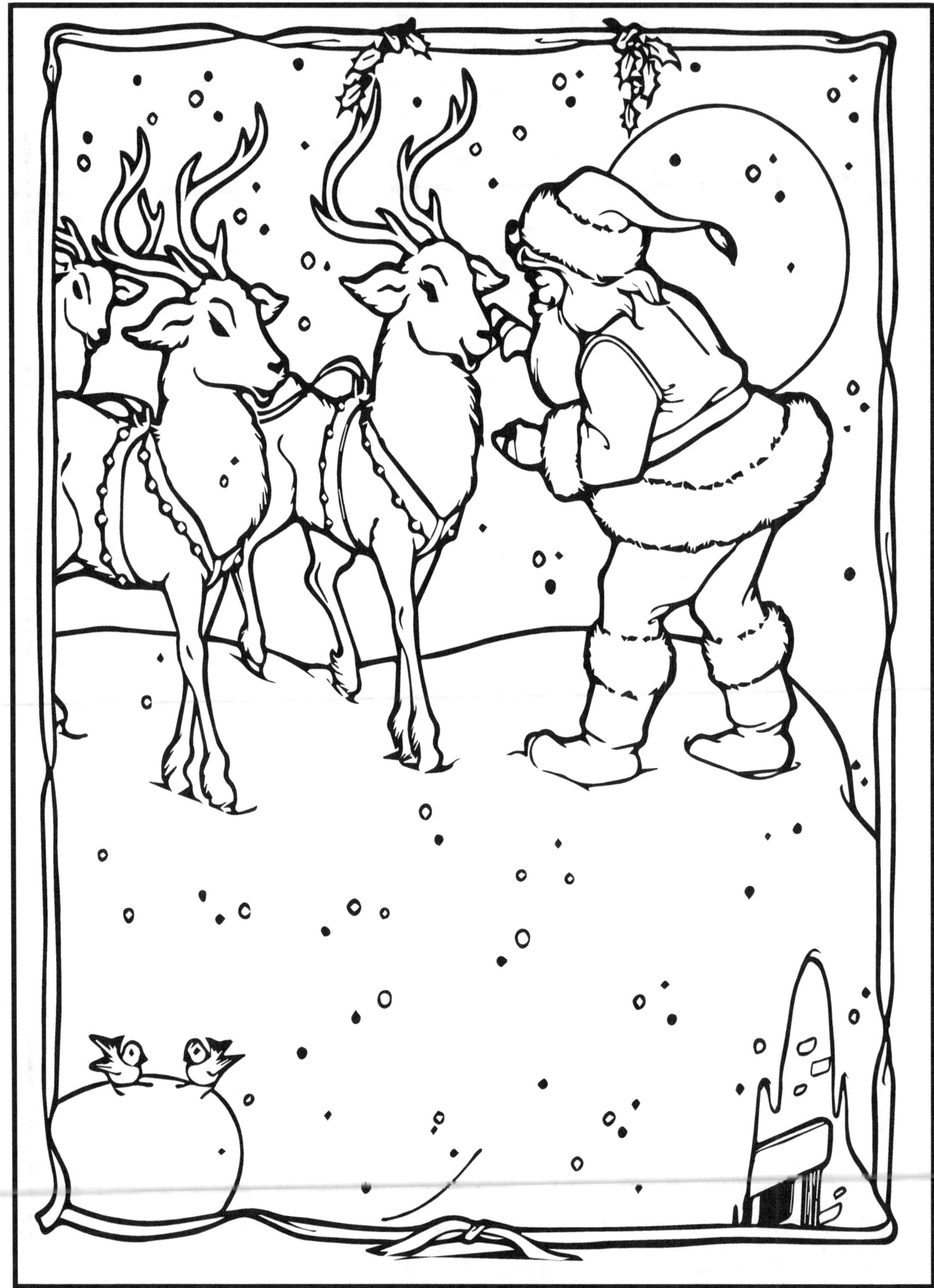

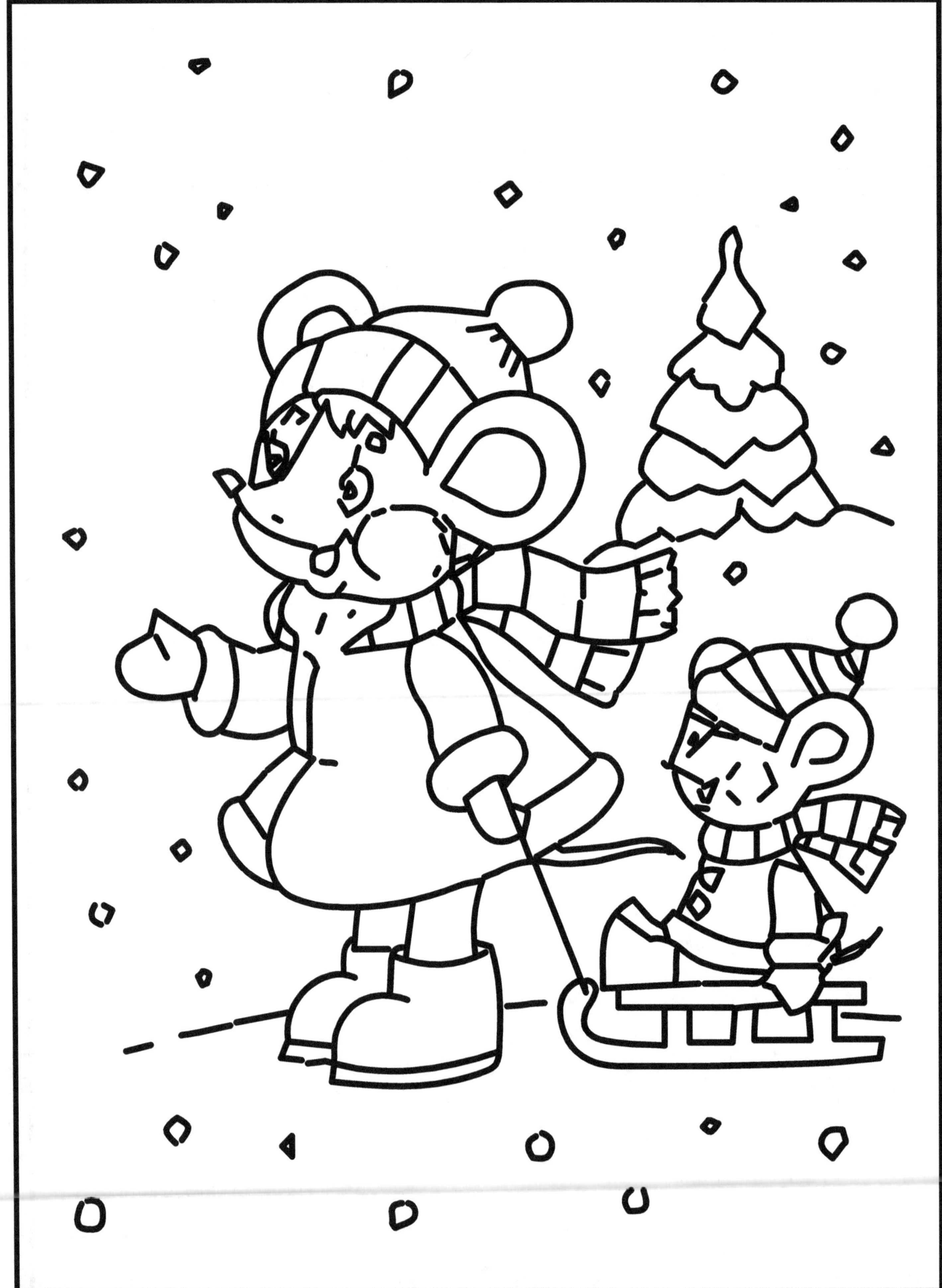

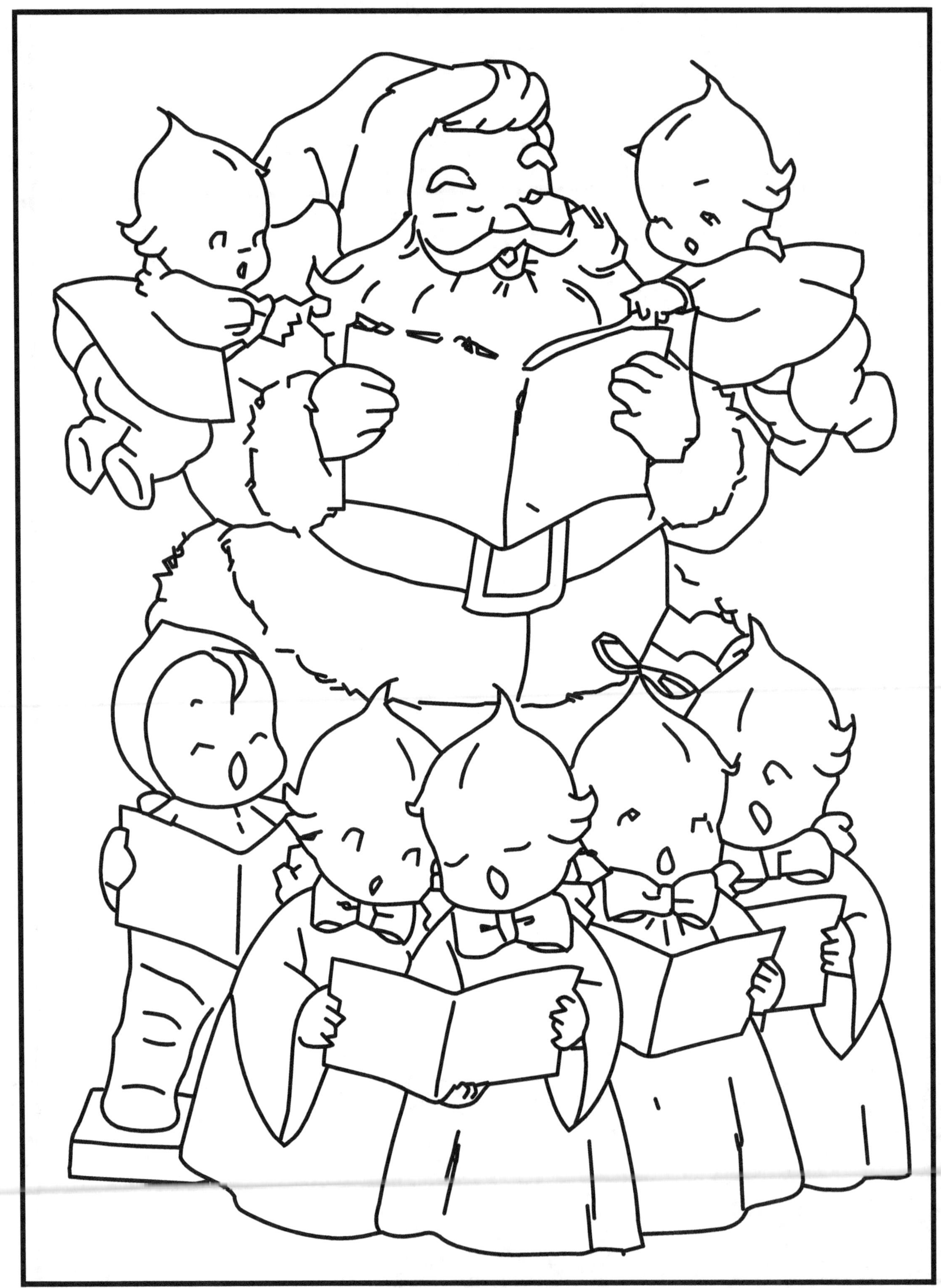

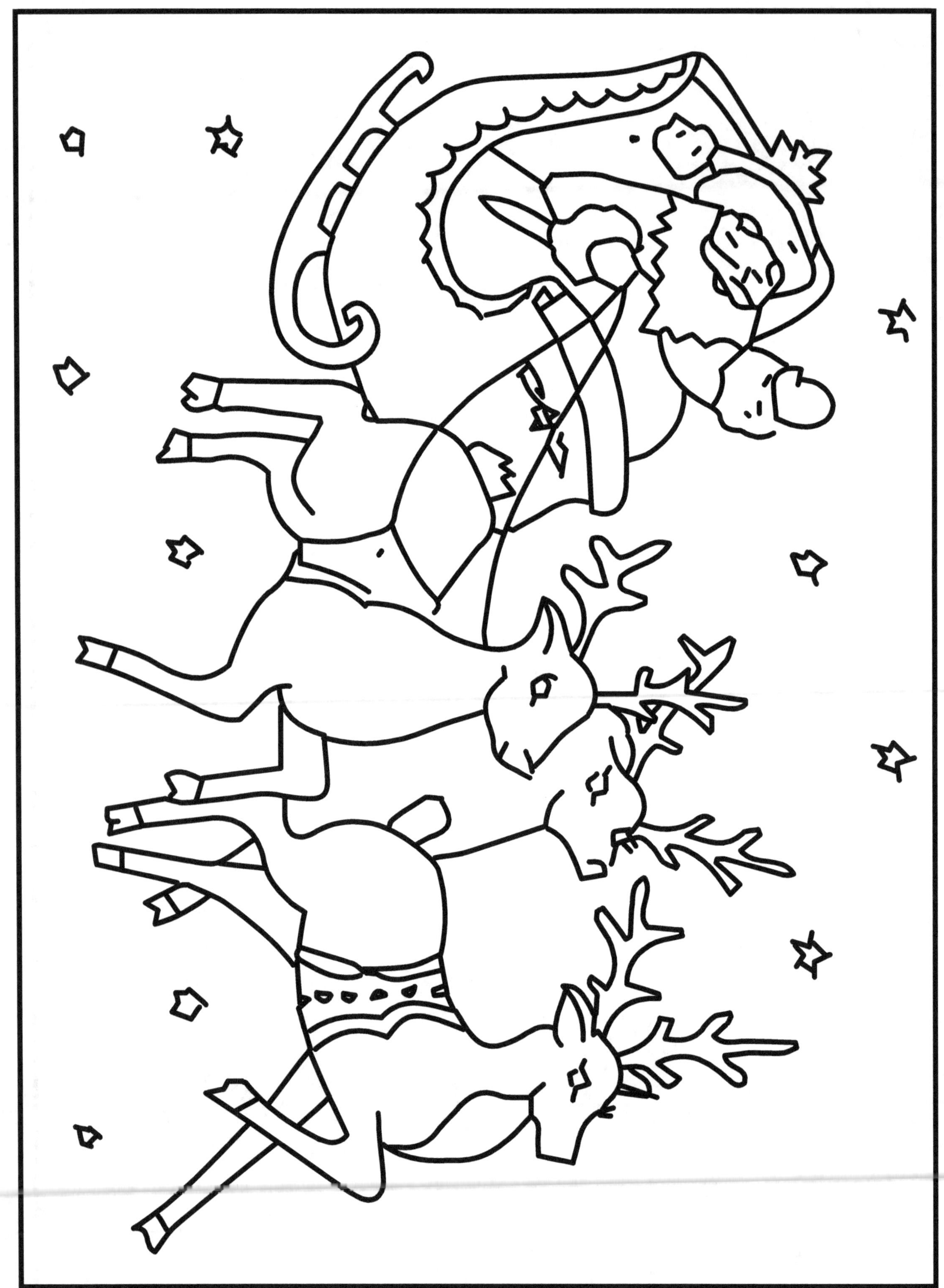

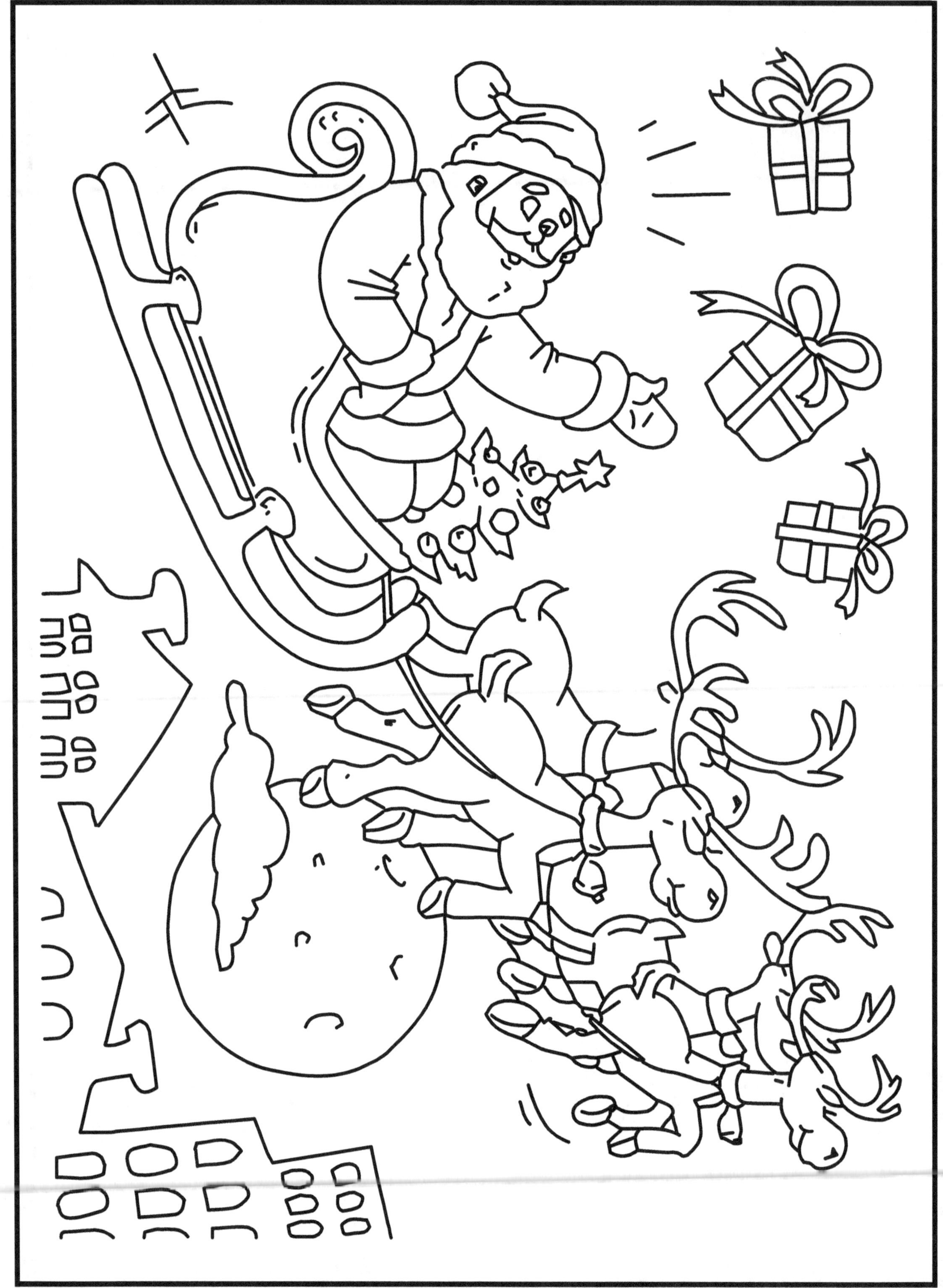

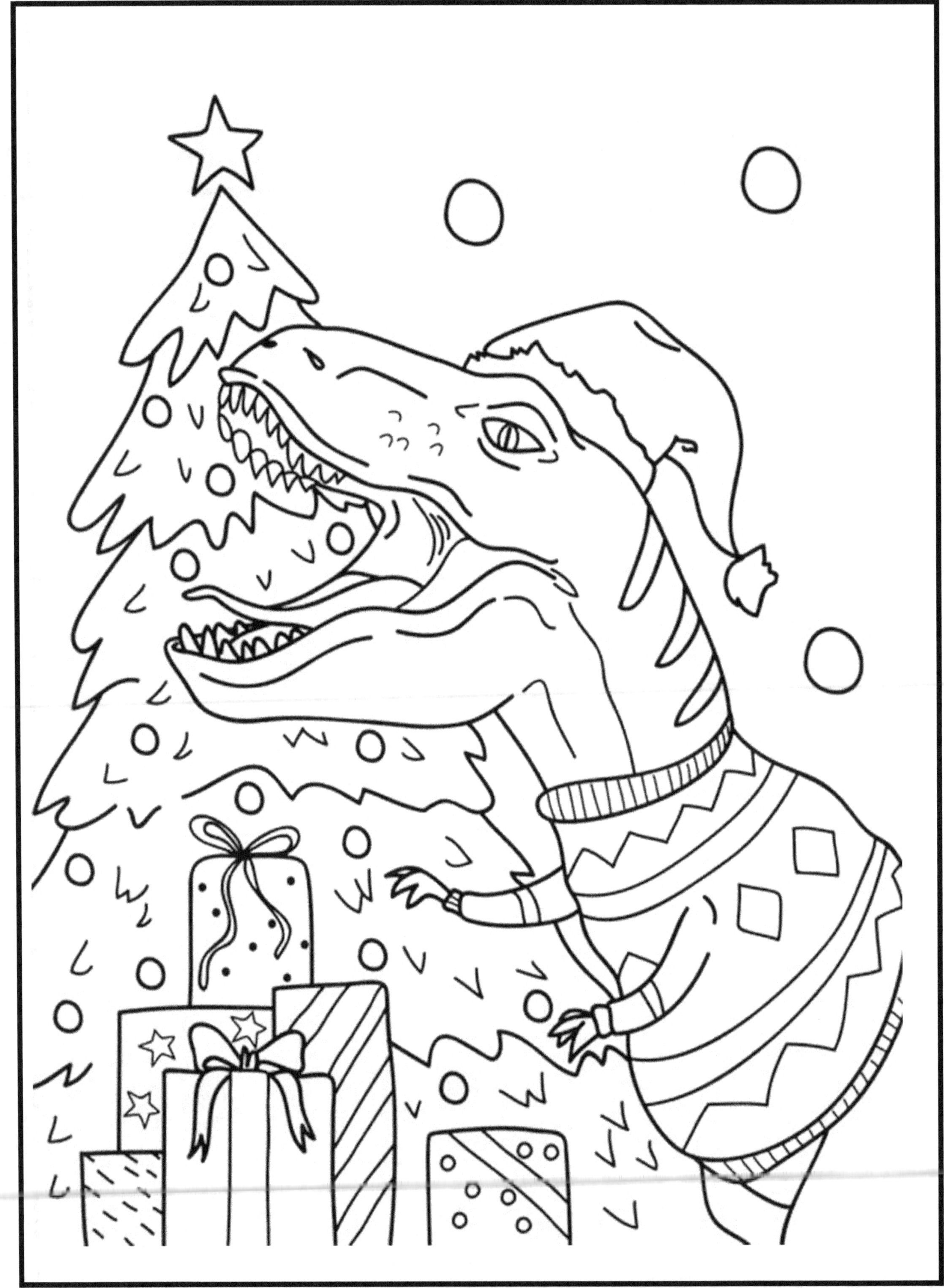

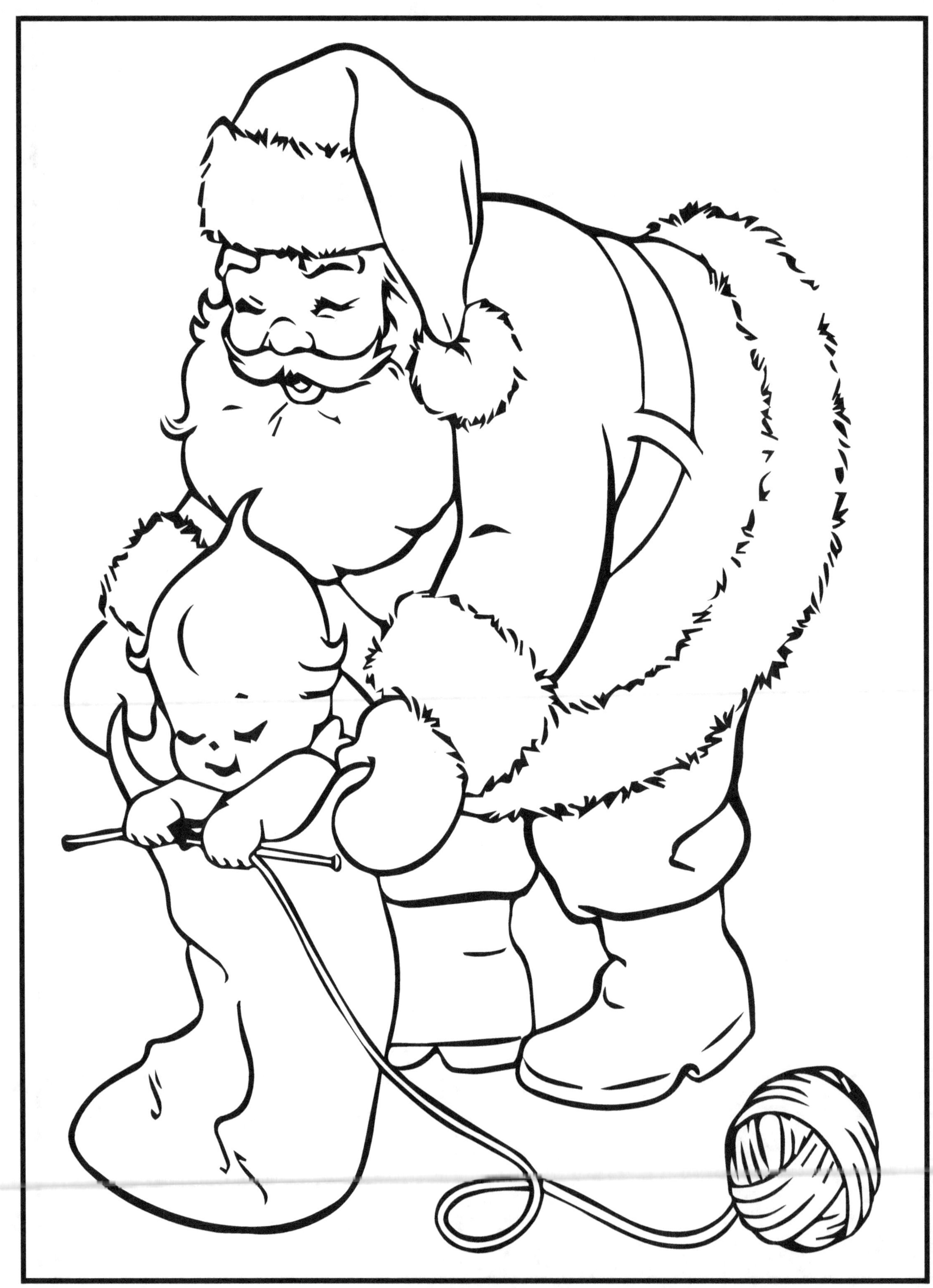

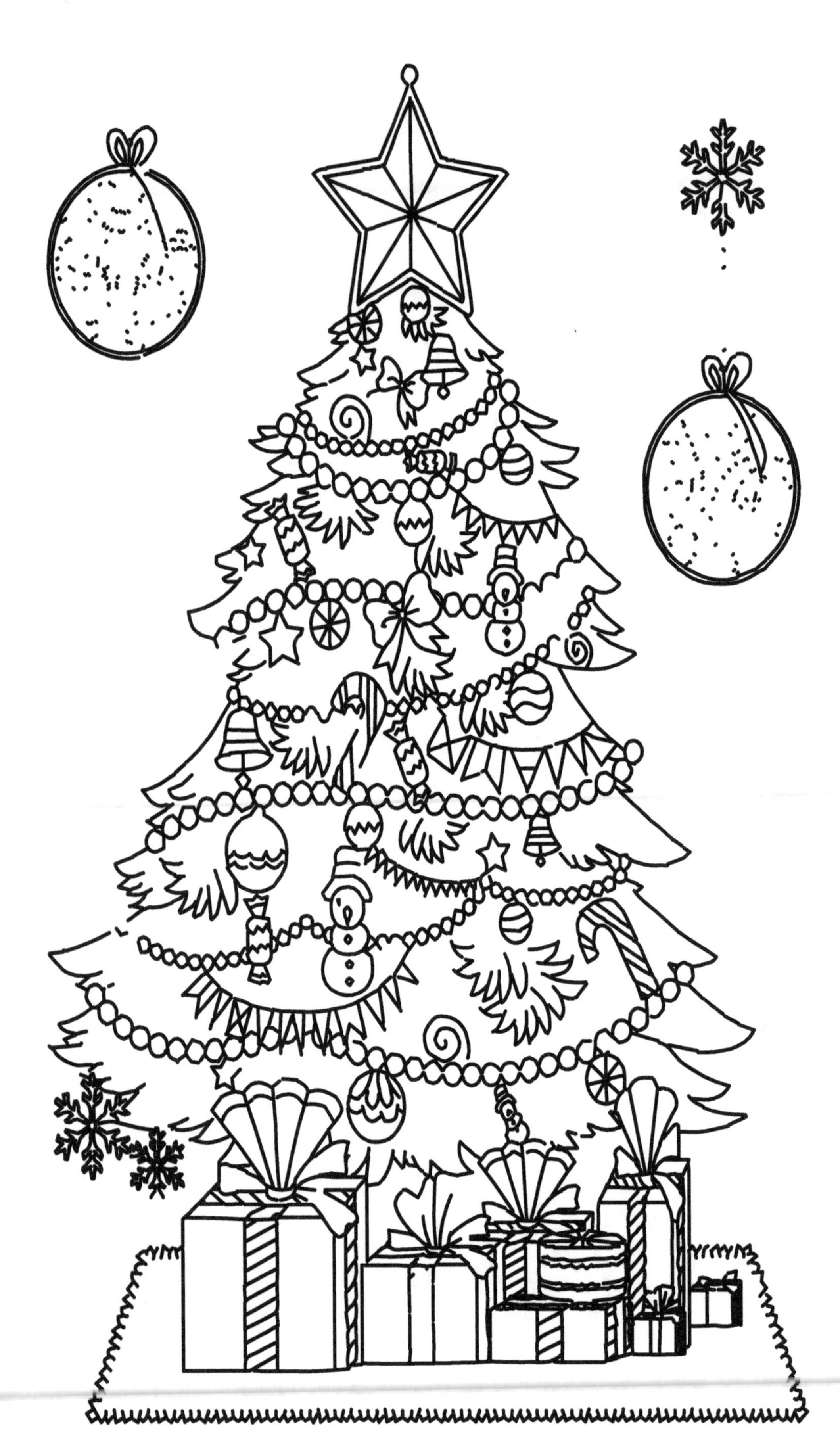

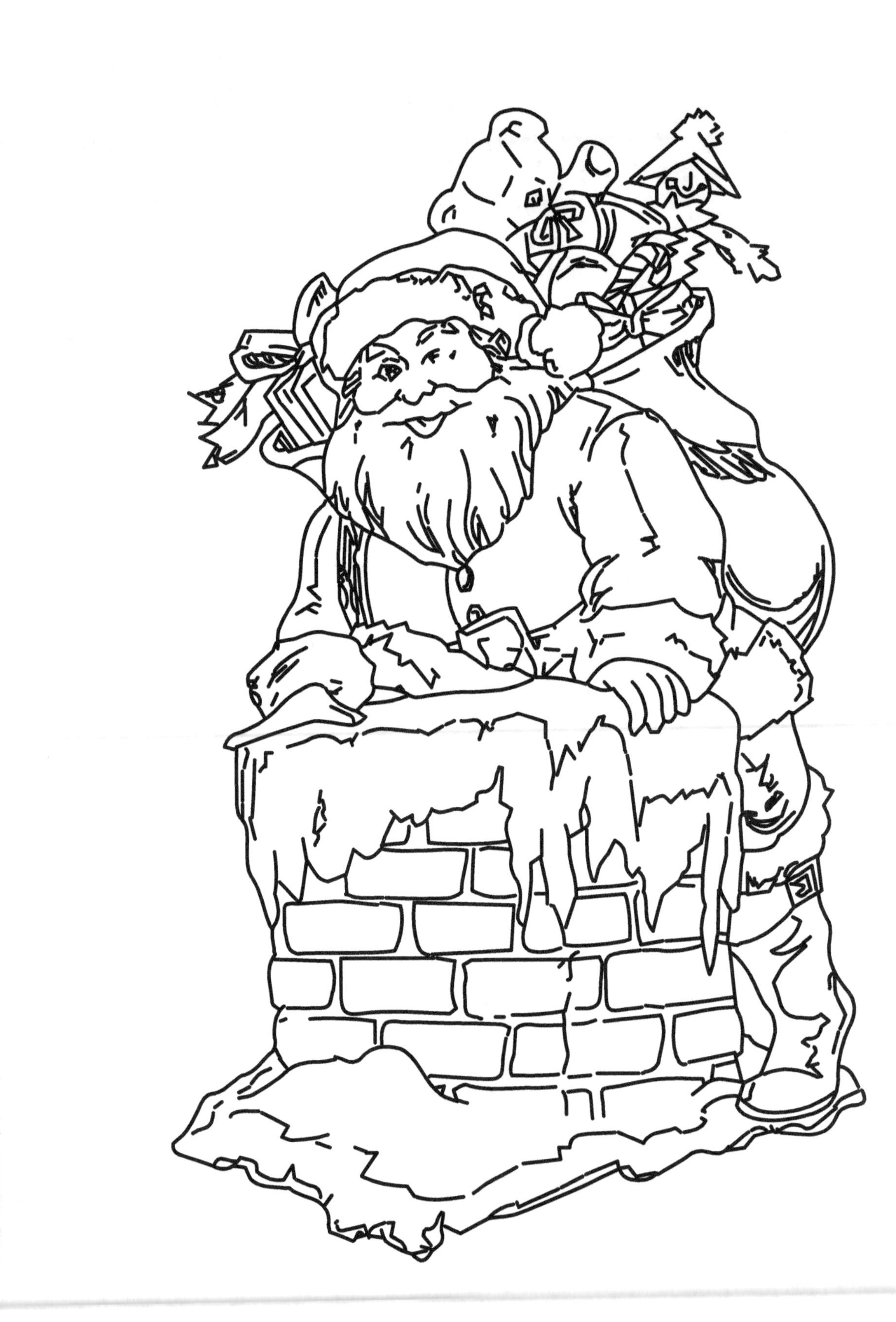

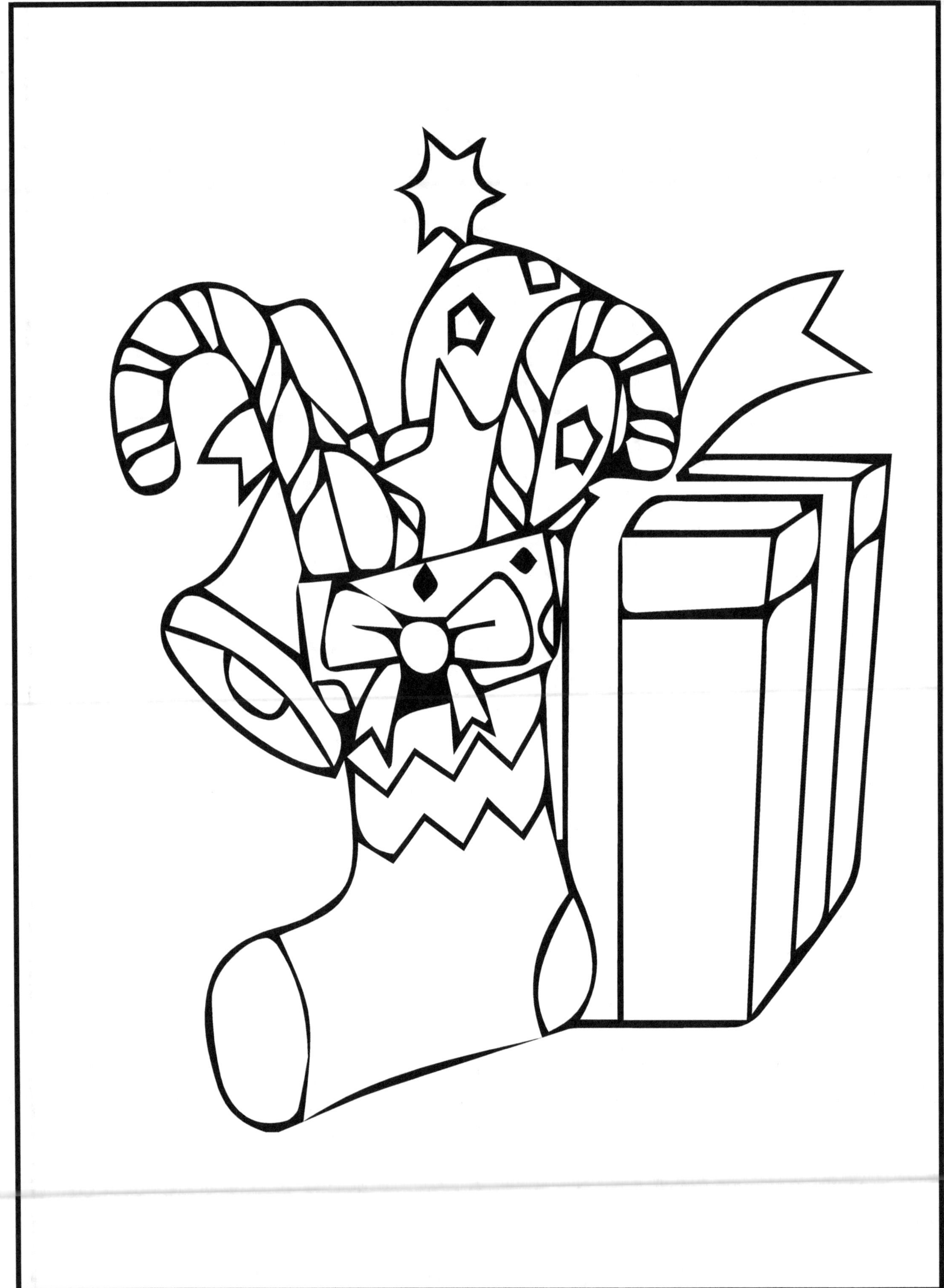

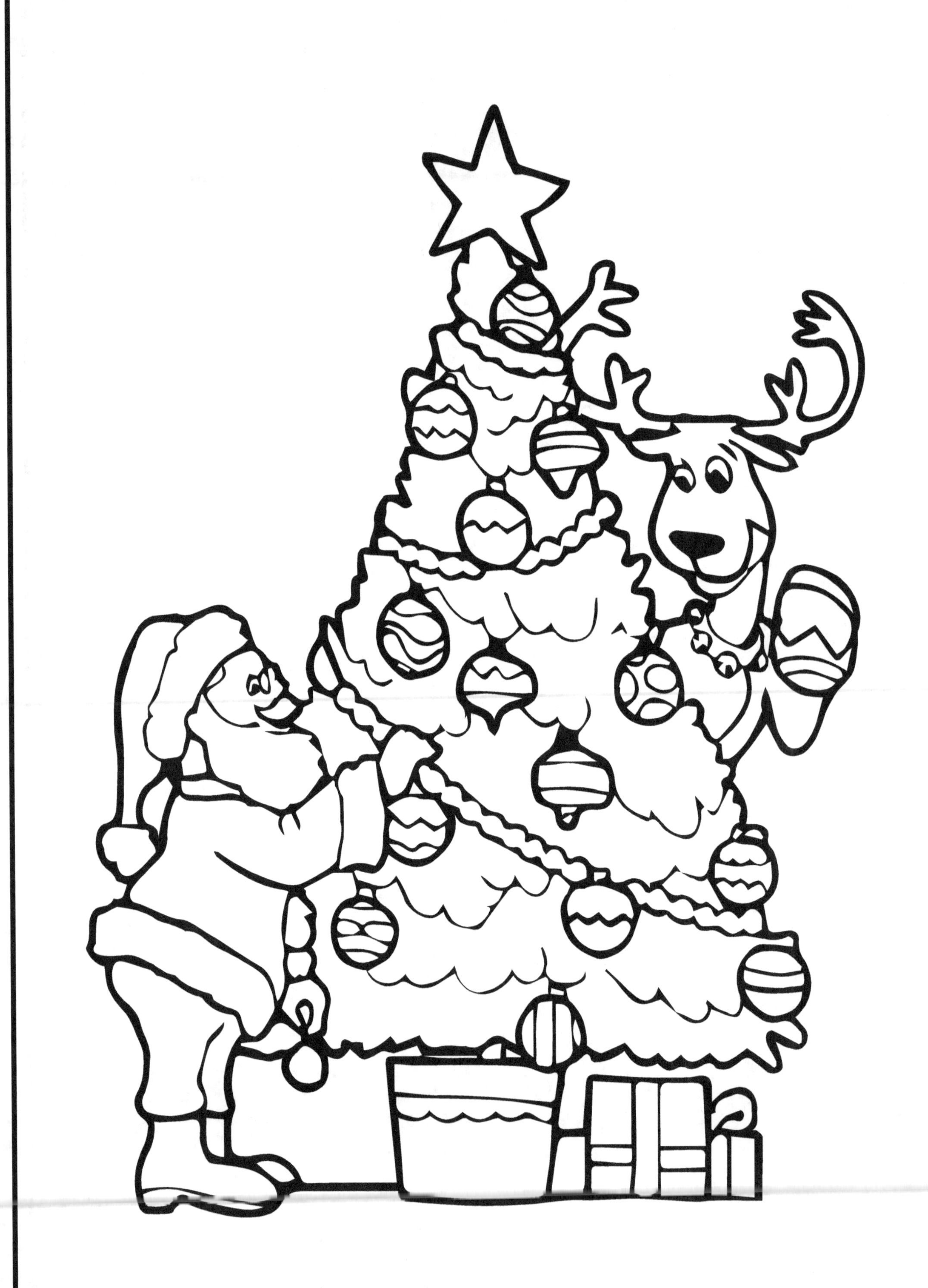

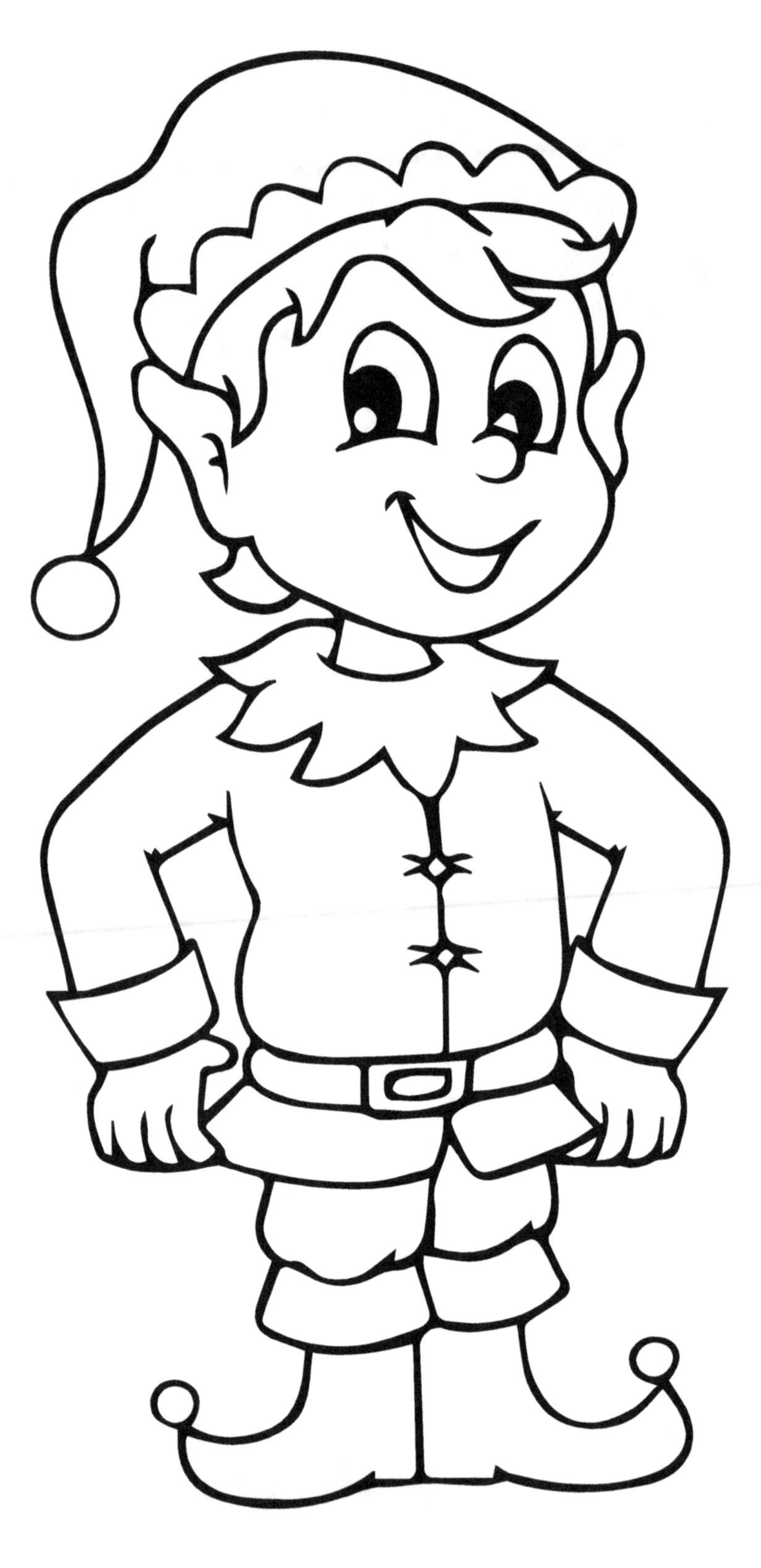

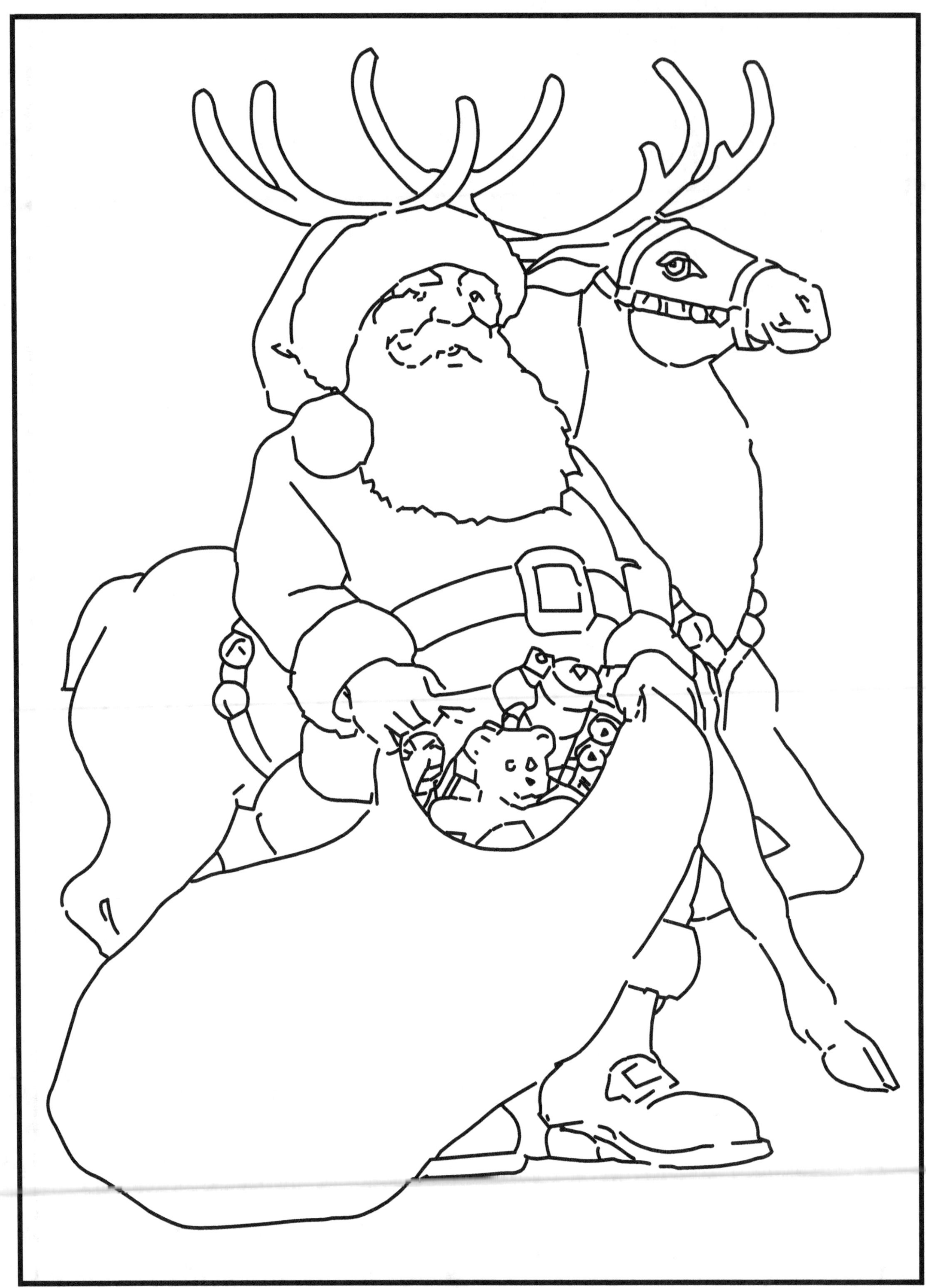

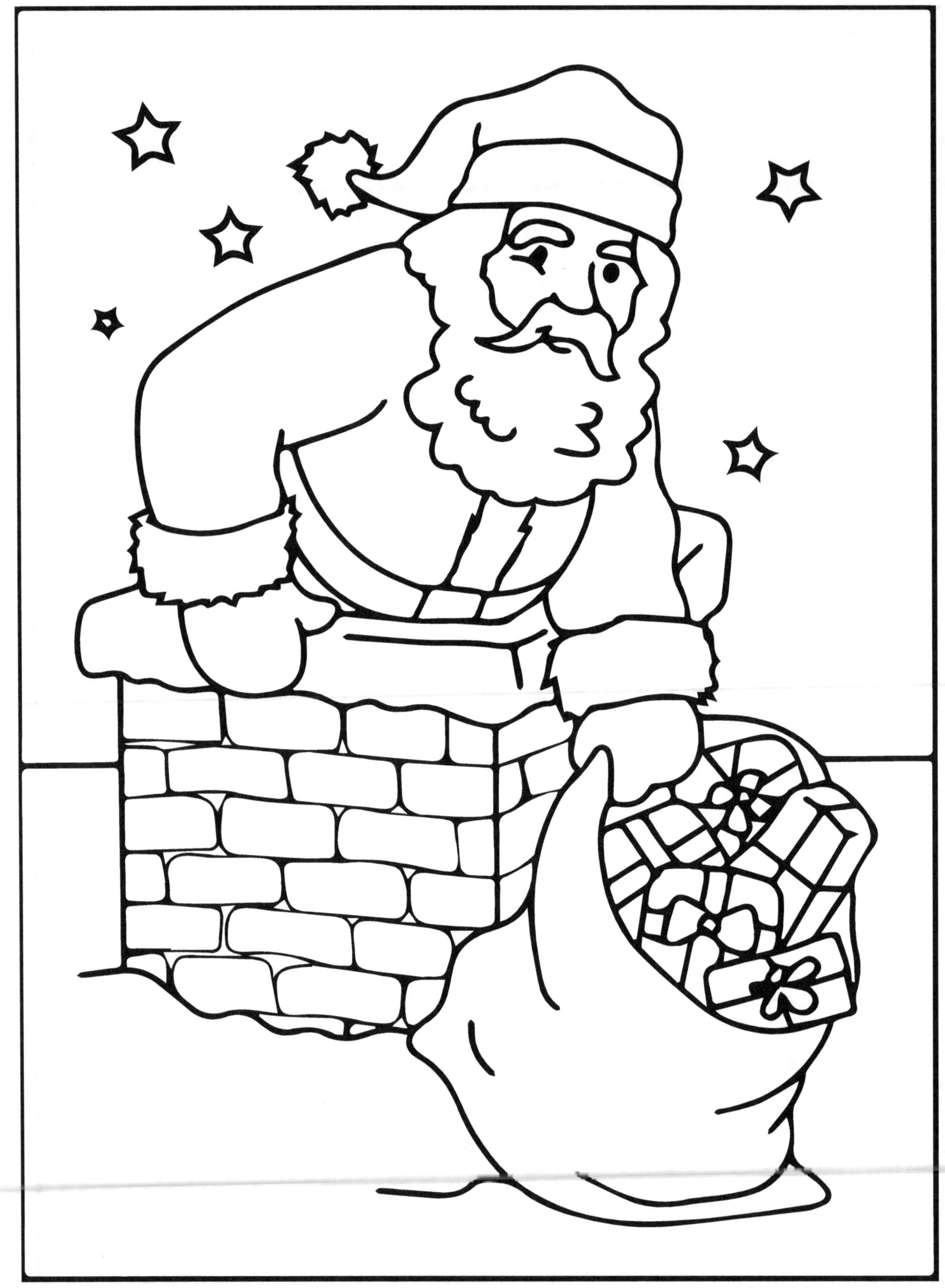

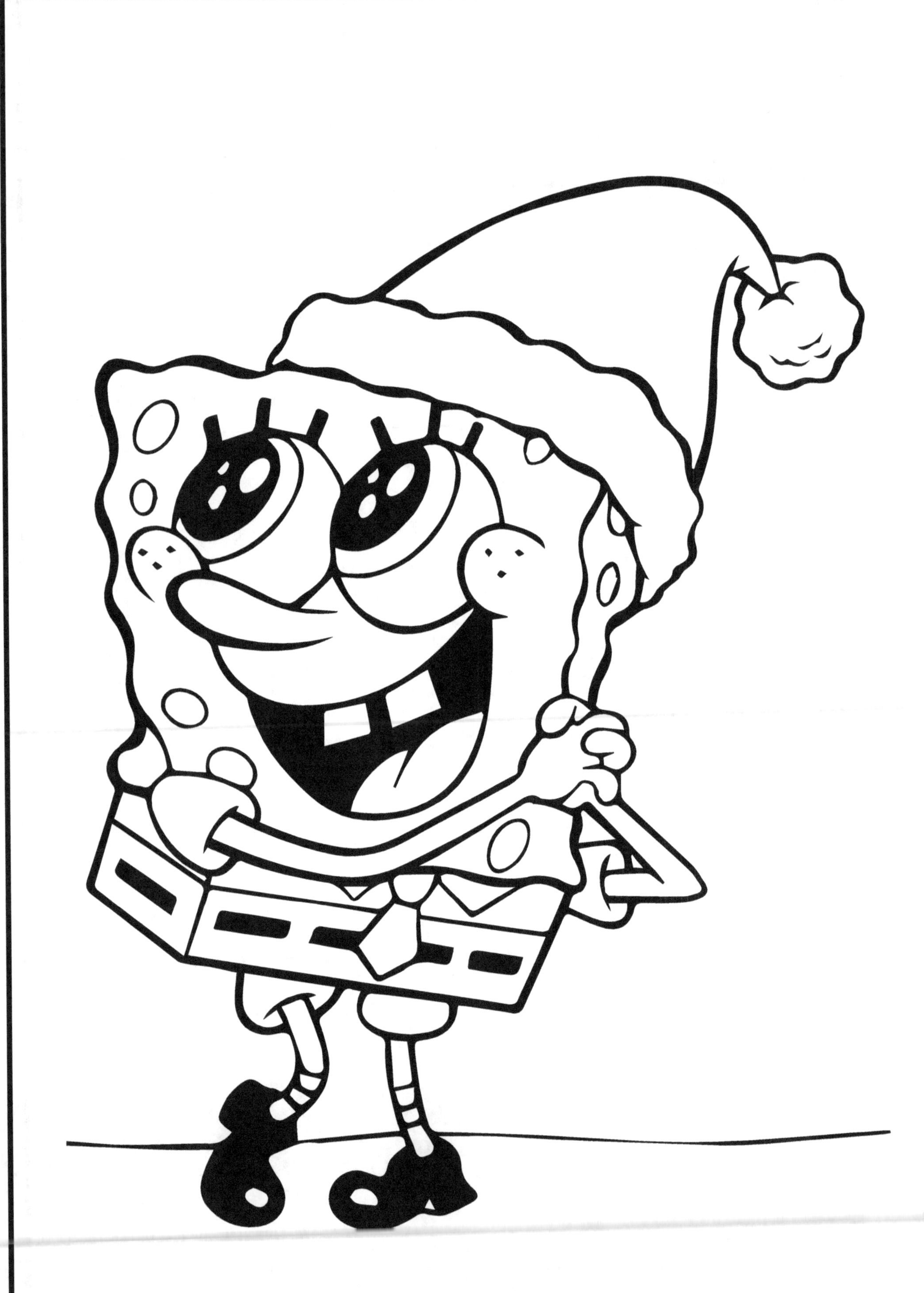

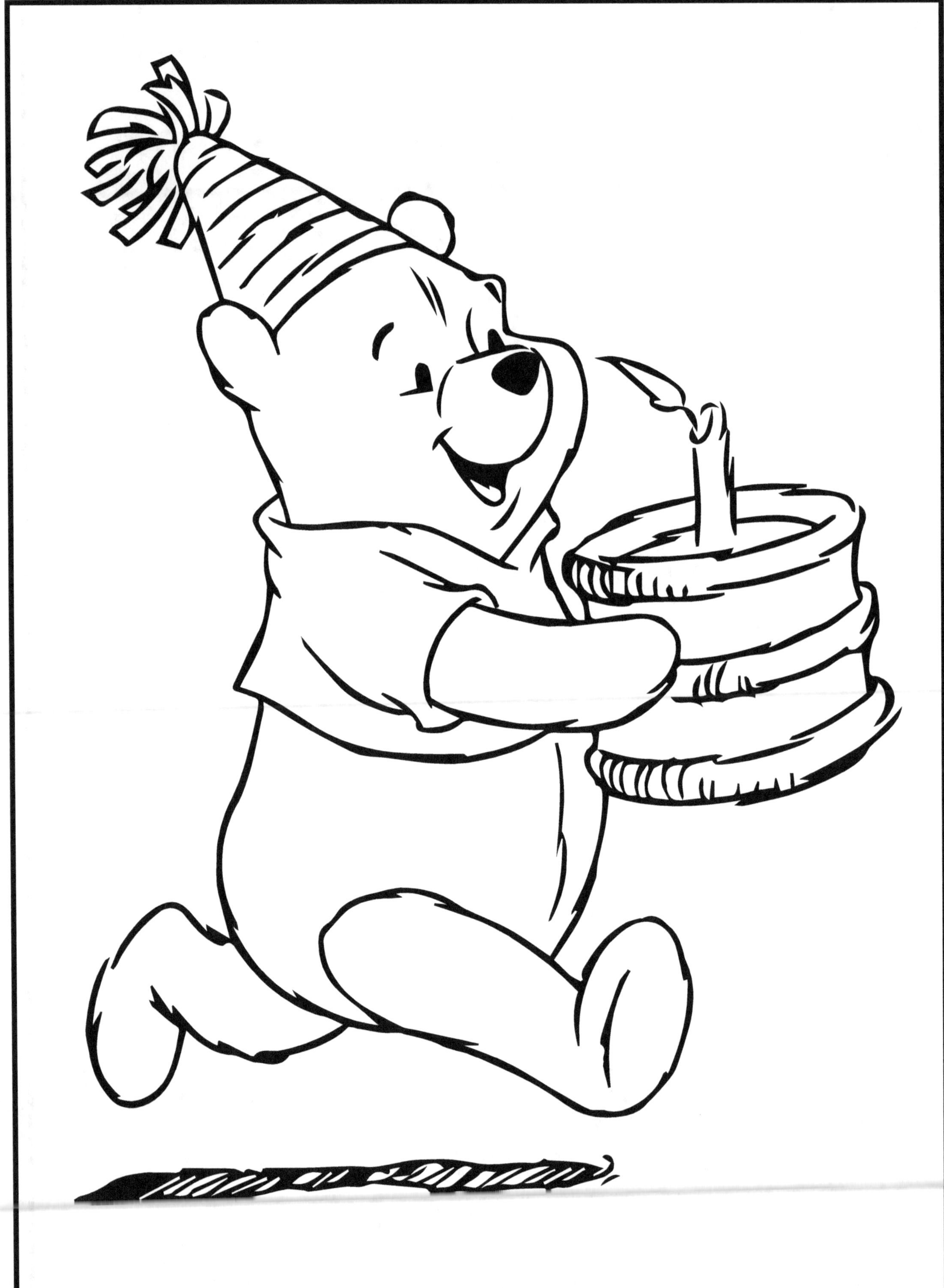

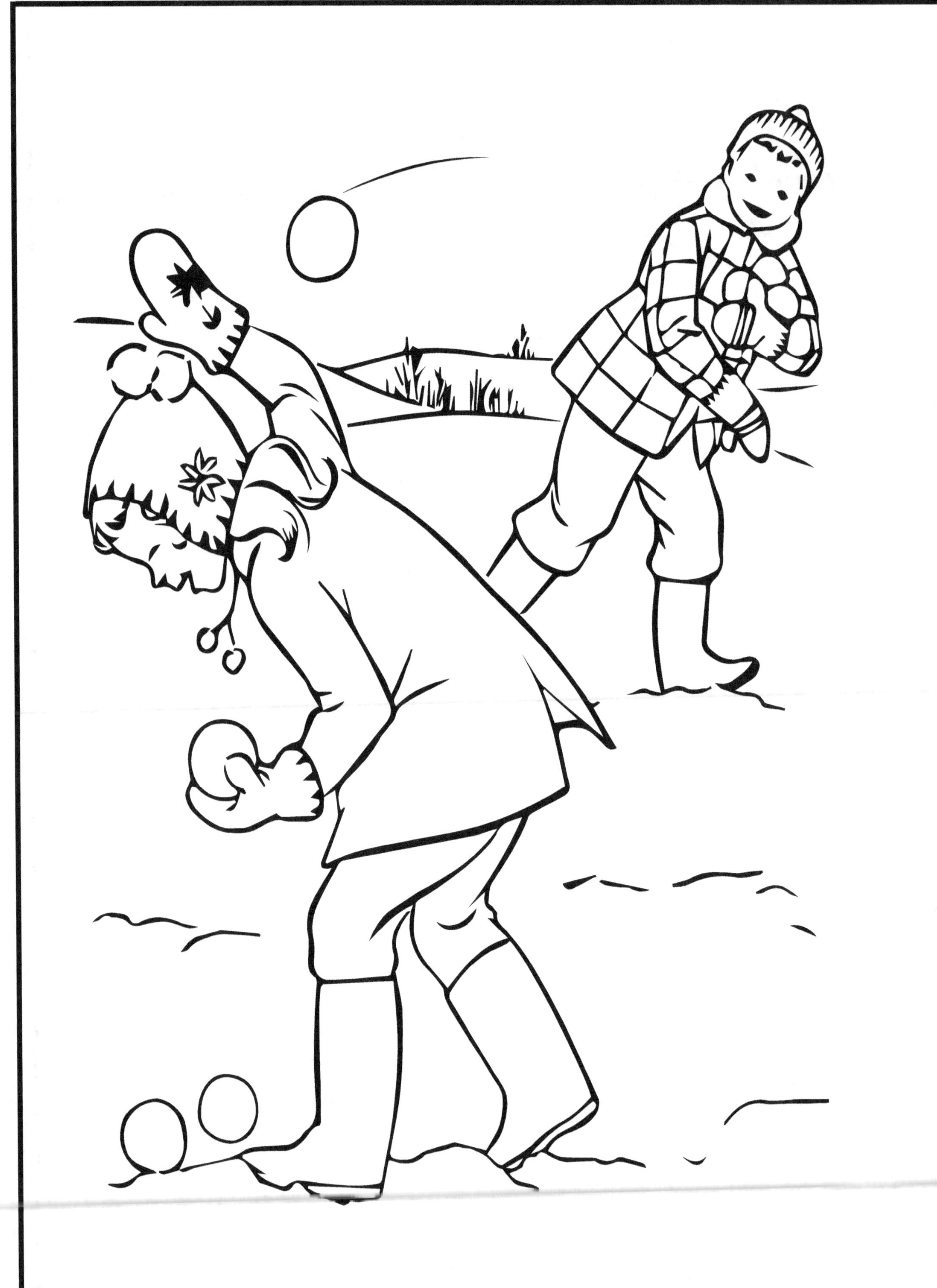

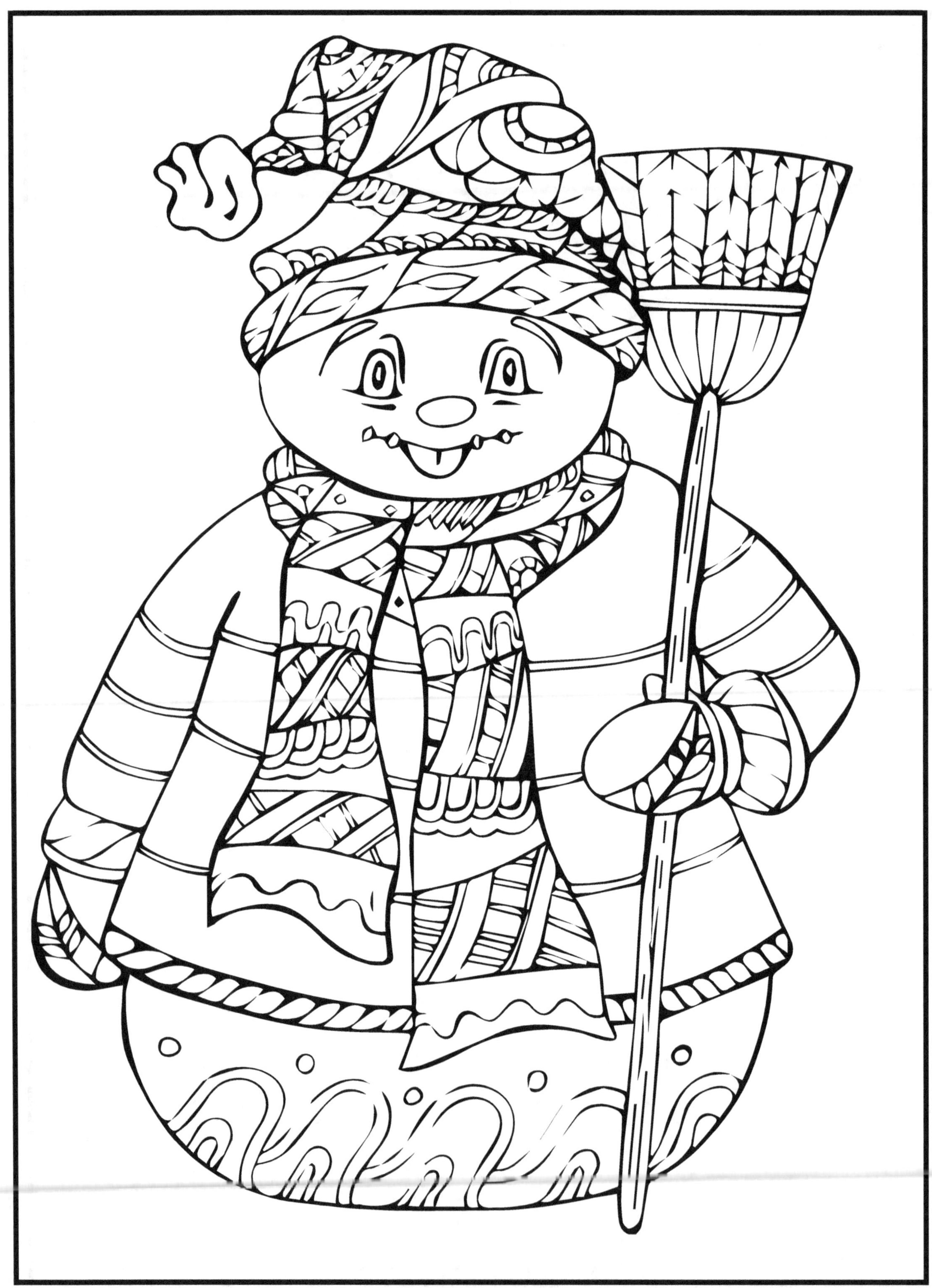

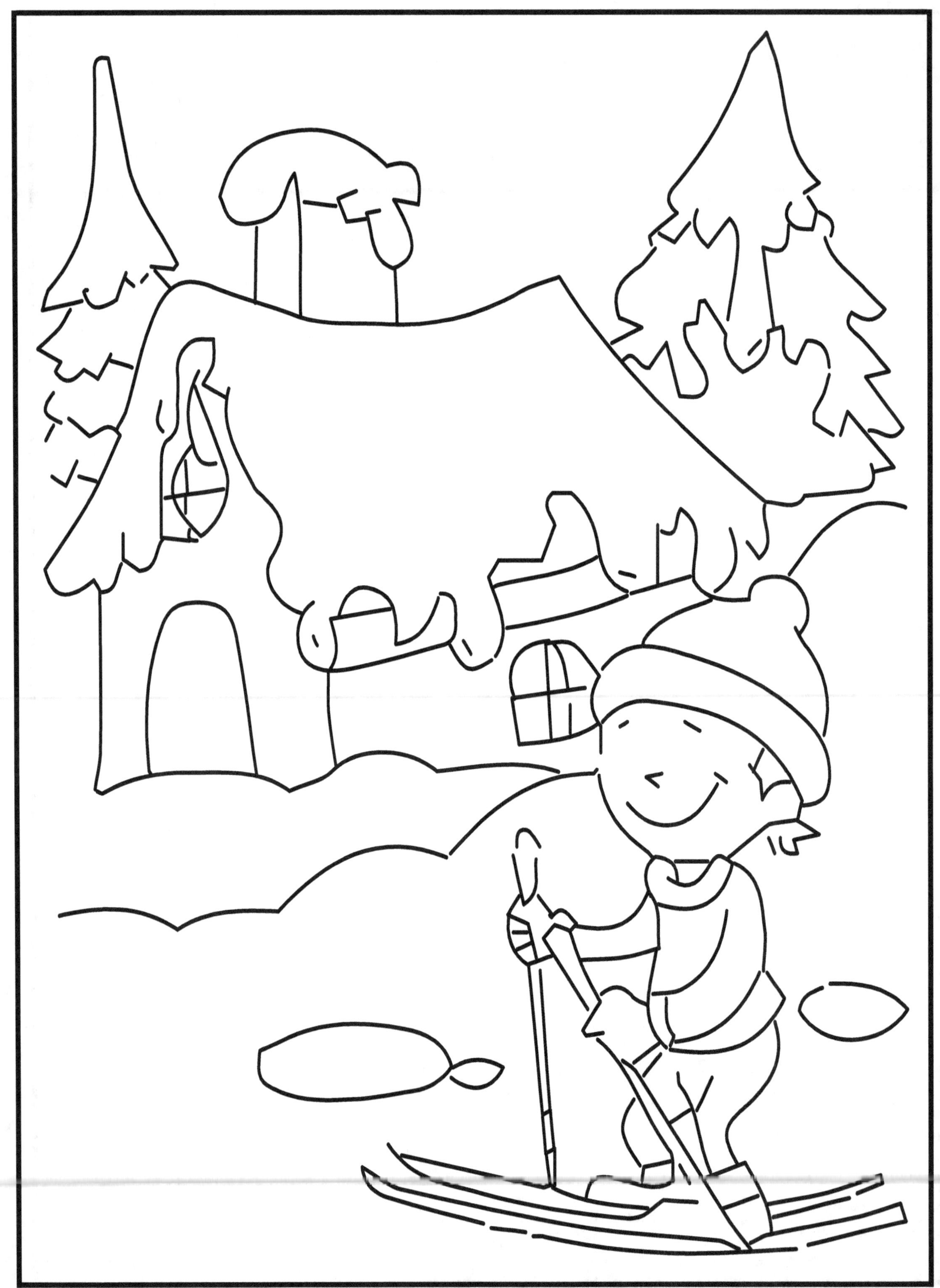

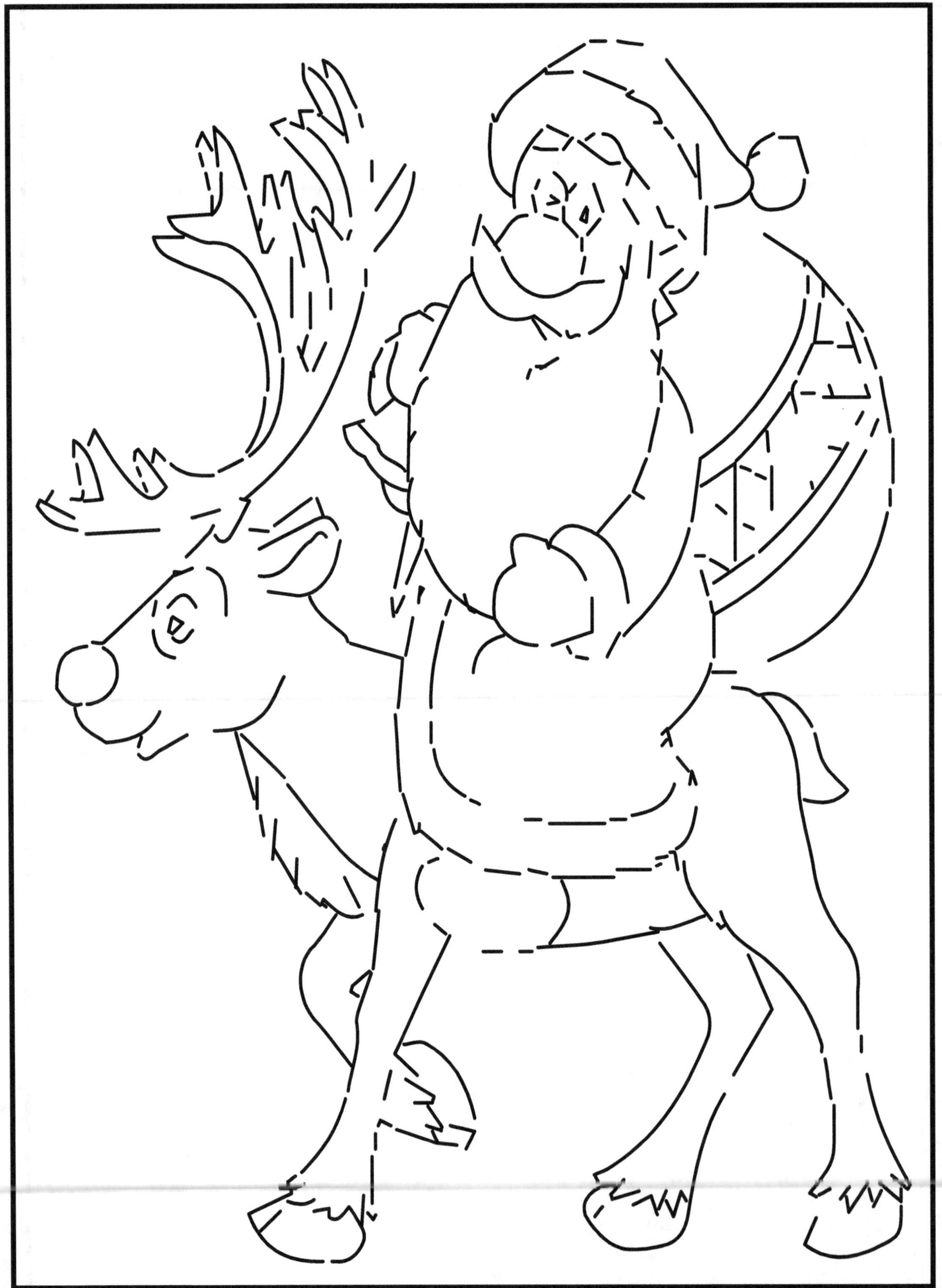

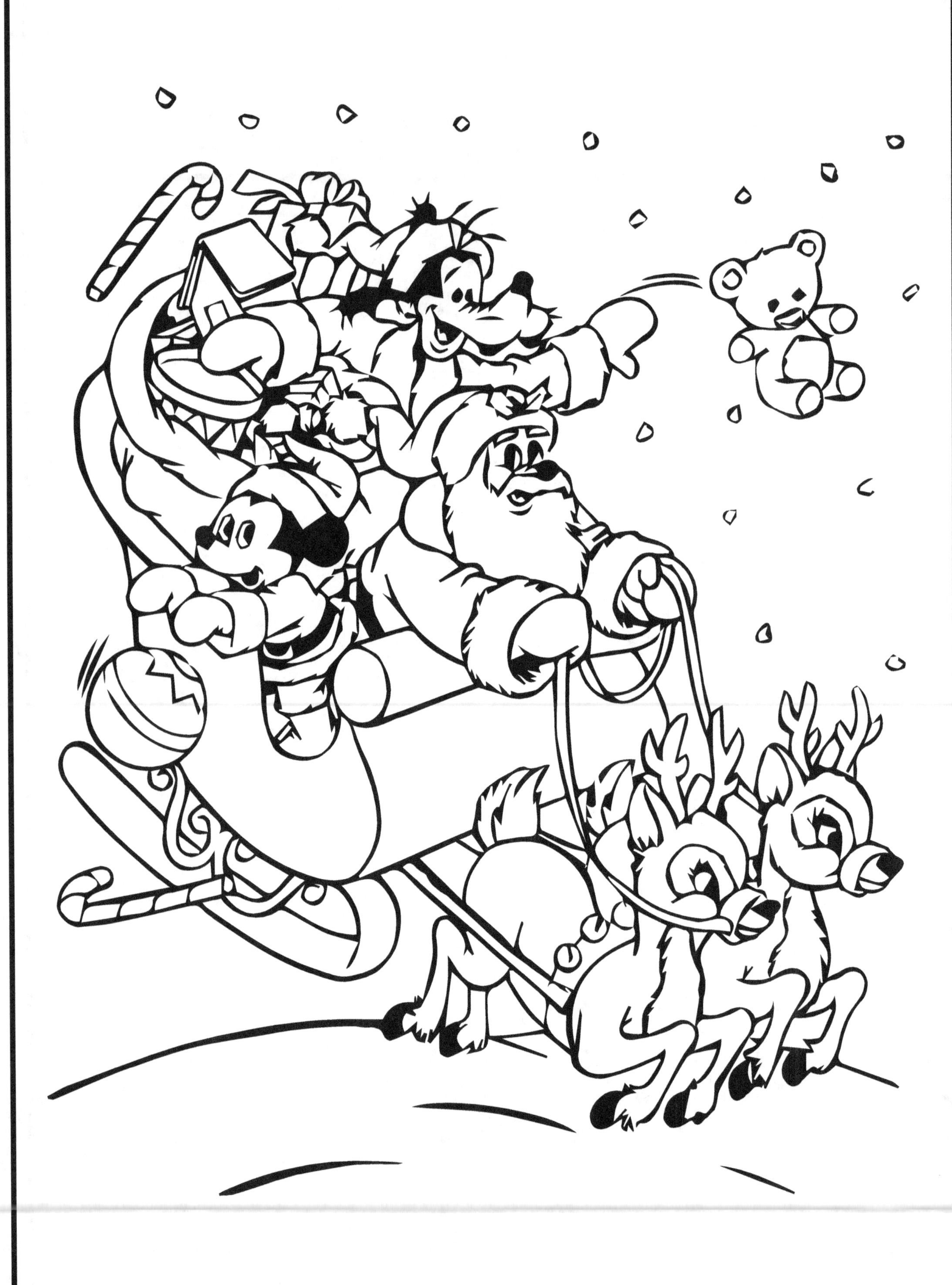

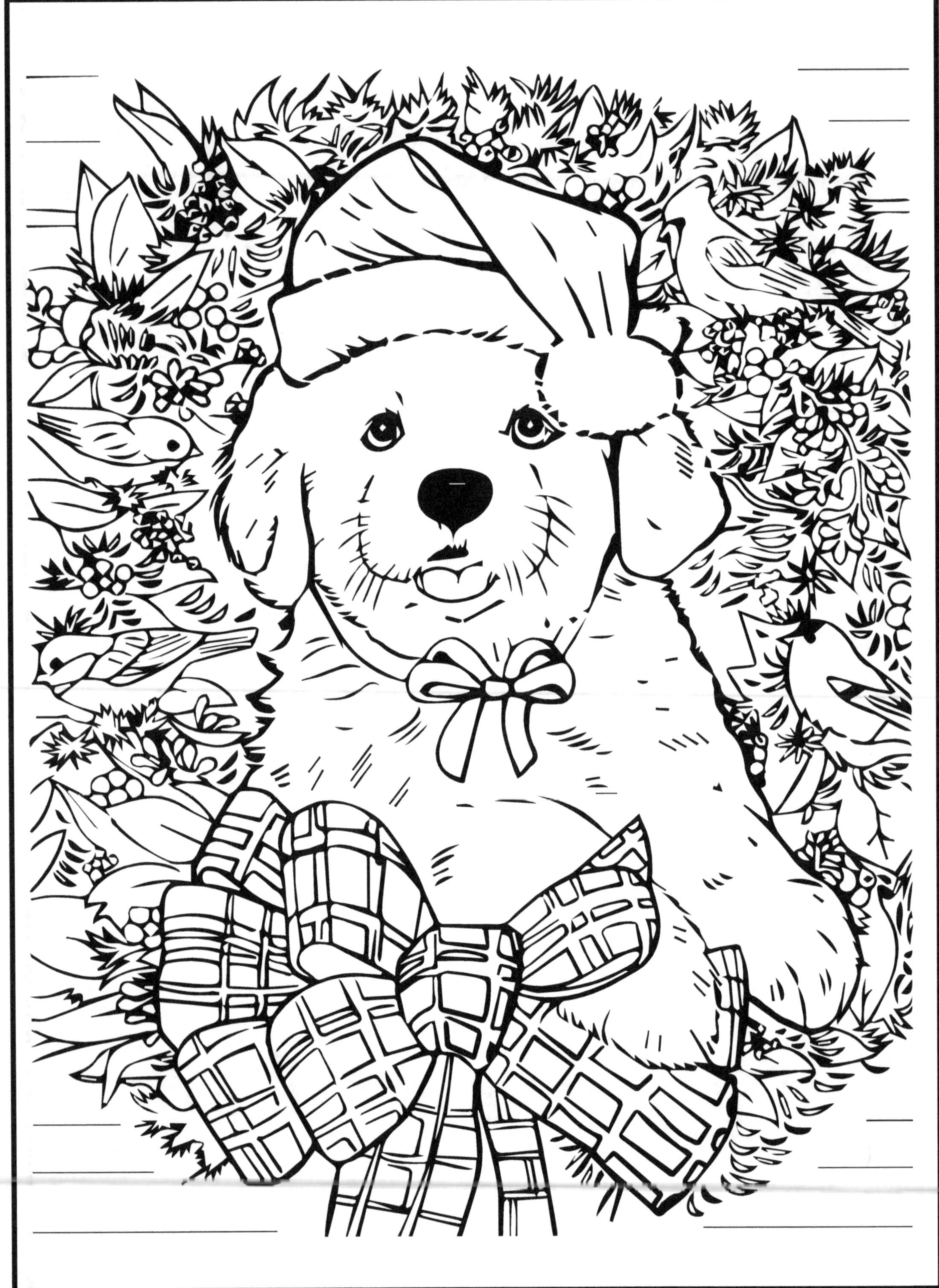

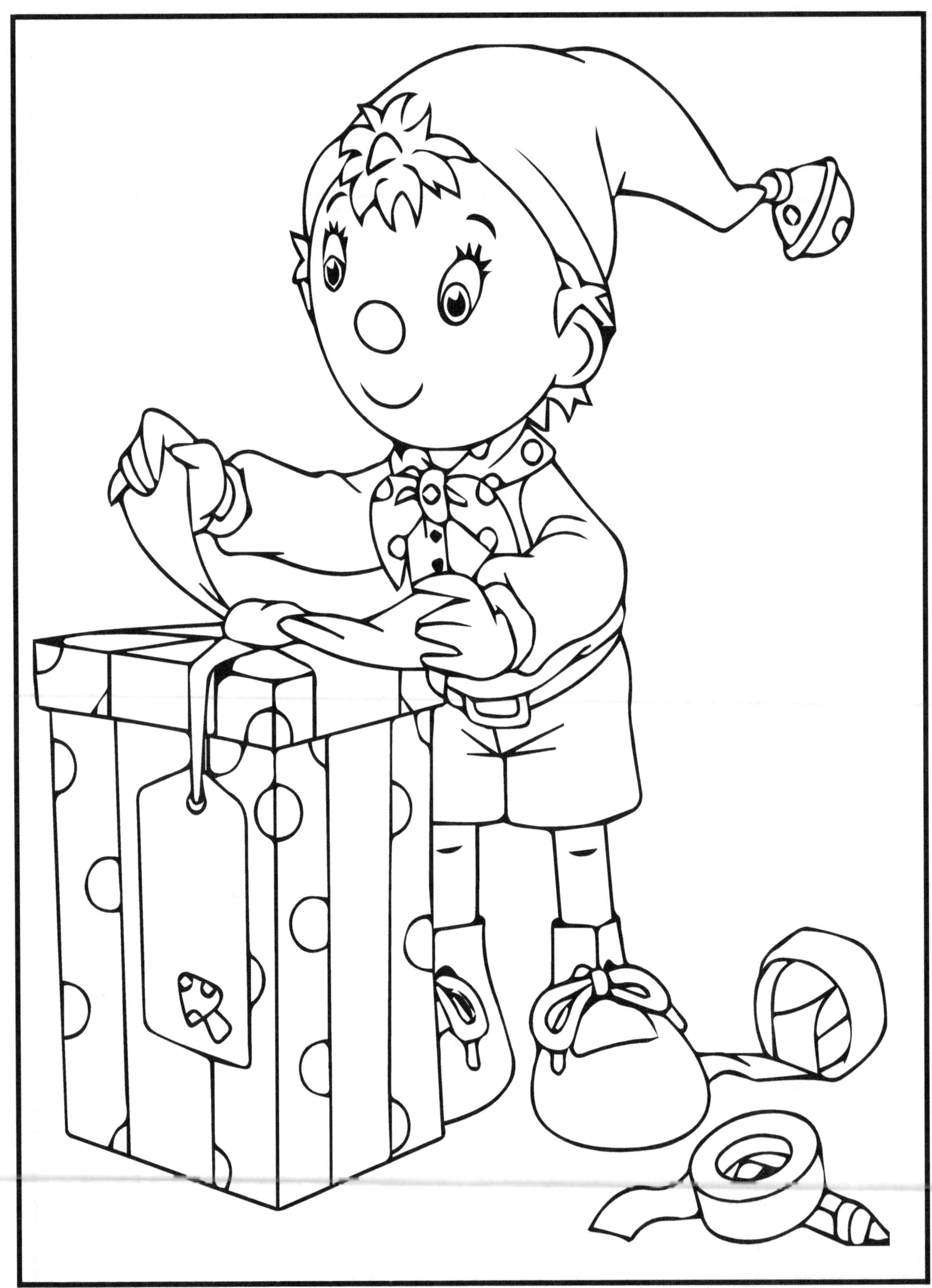

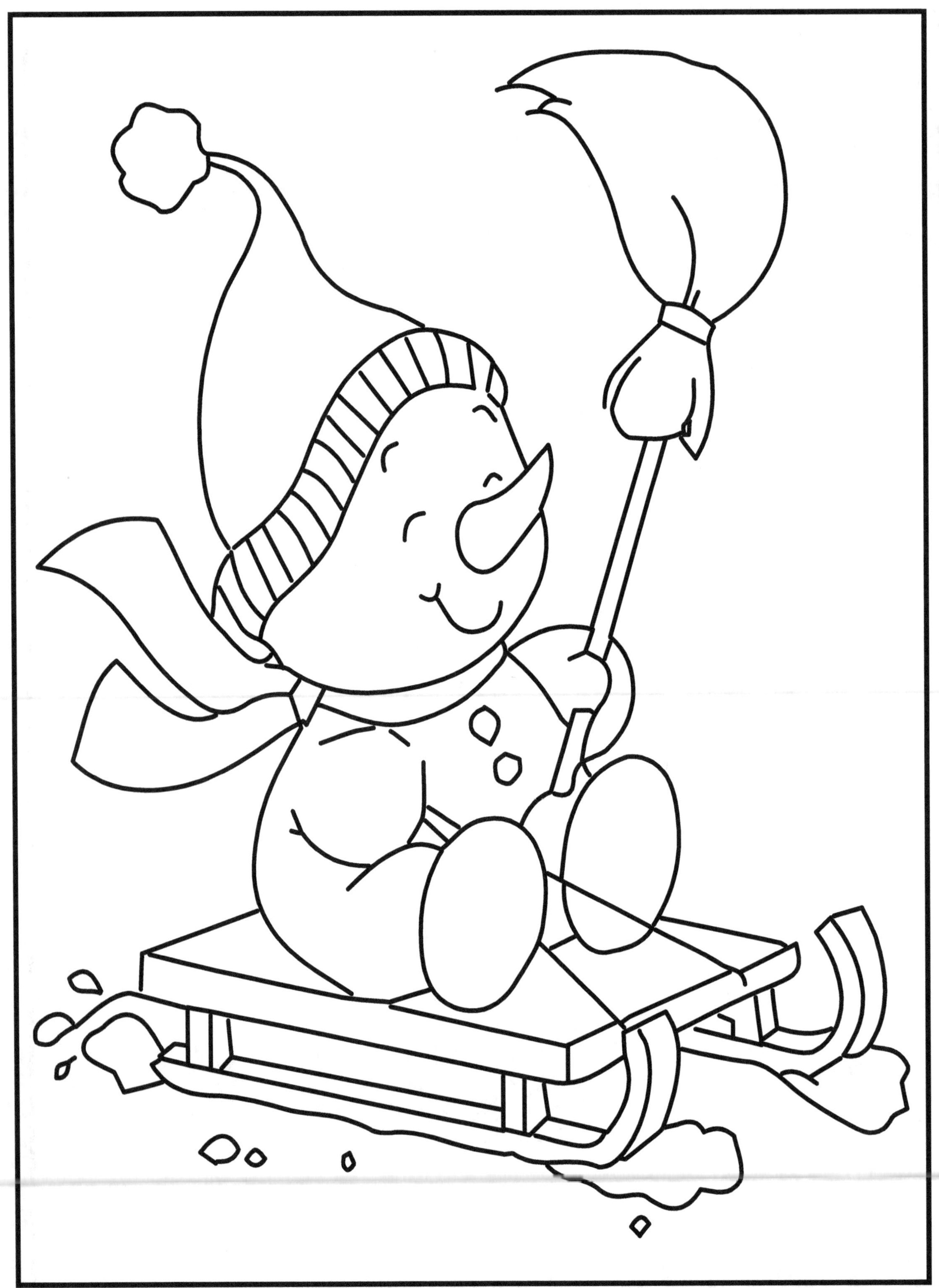

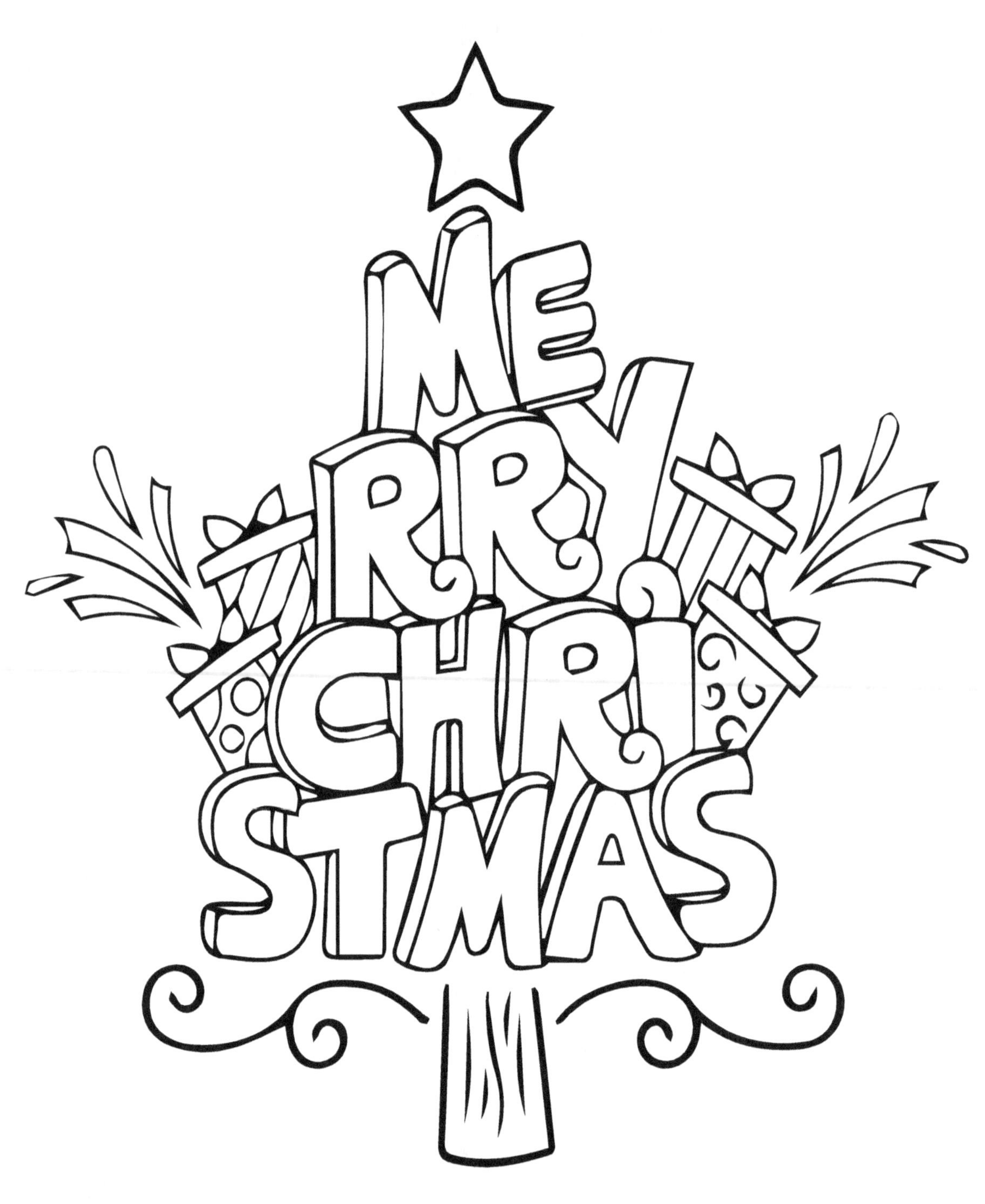

MERRY CHRISTMAS

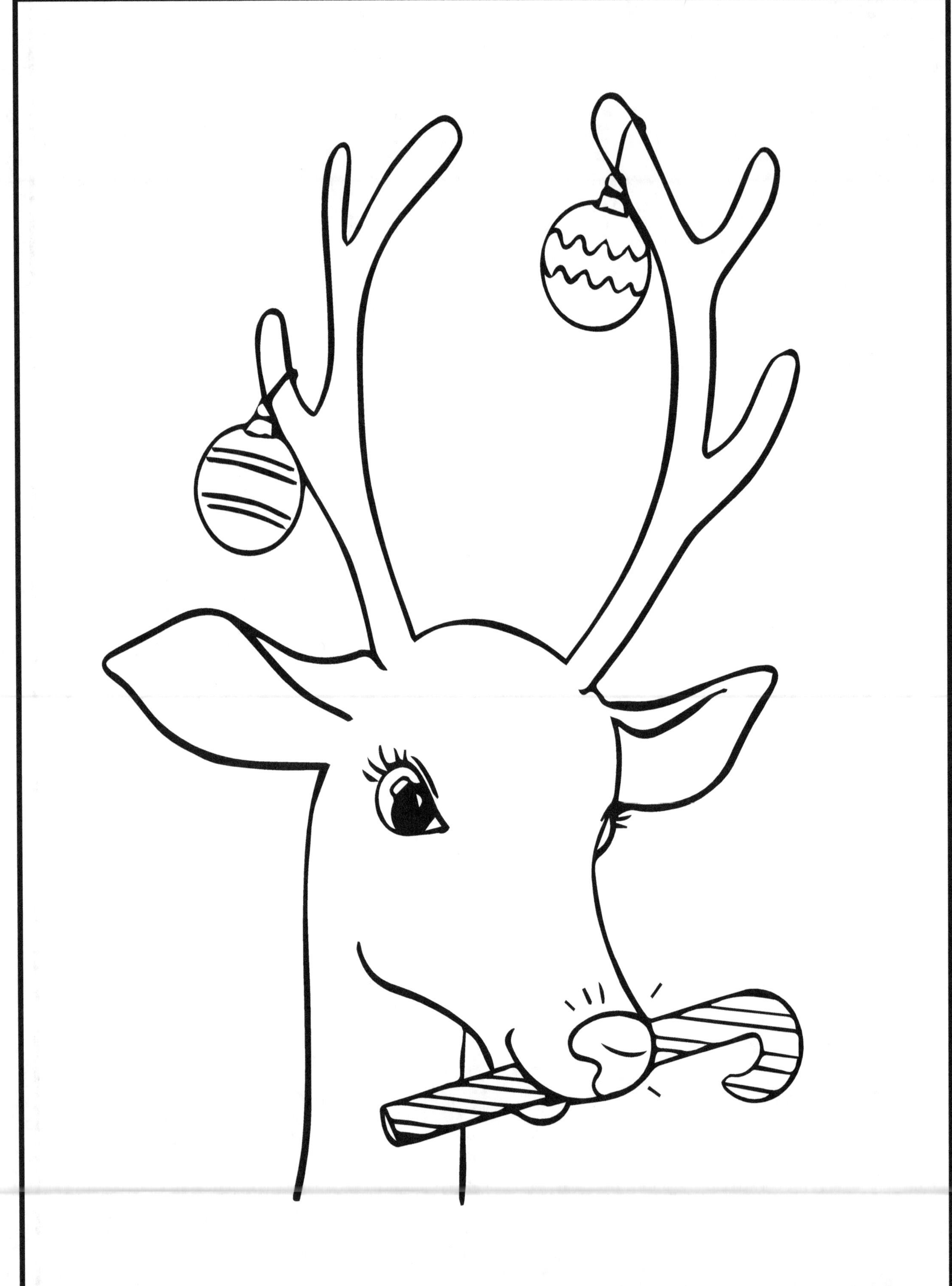

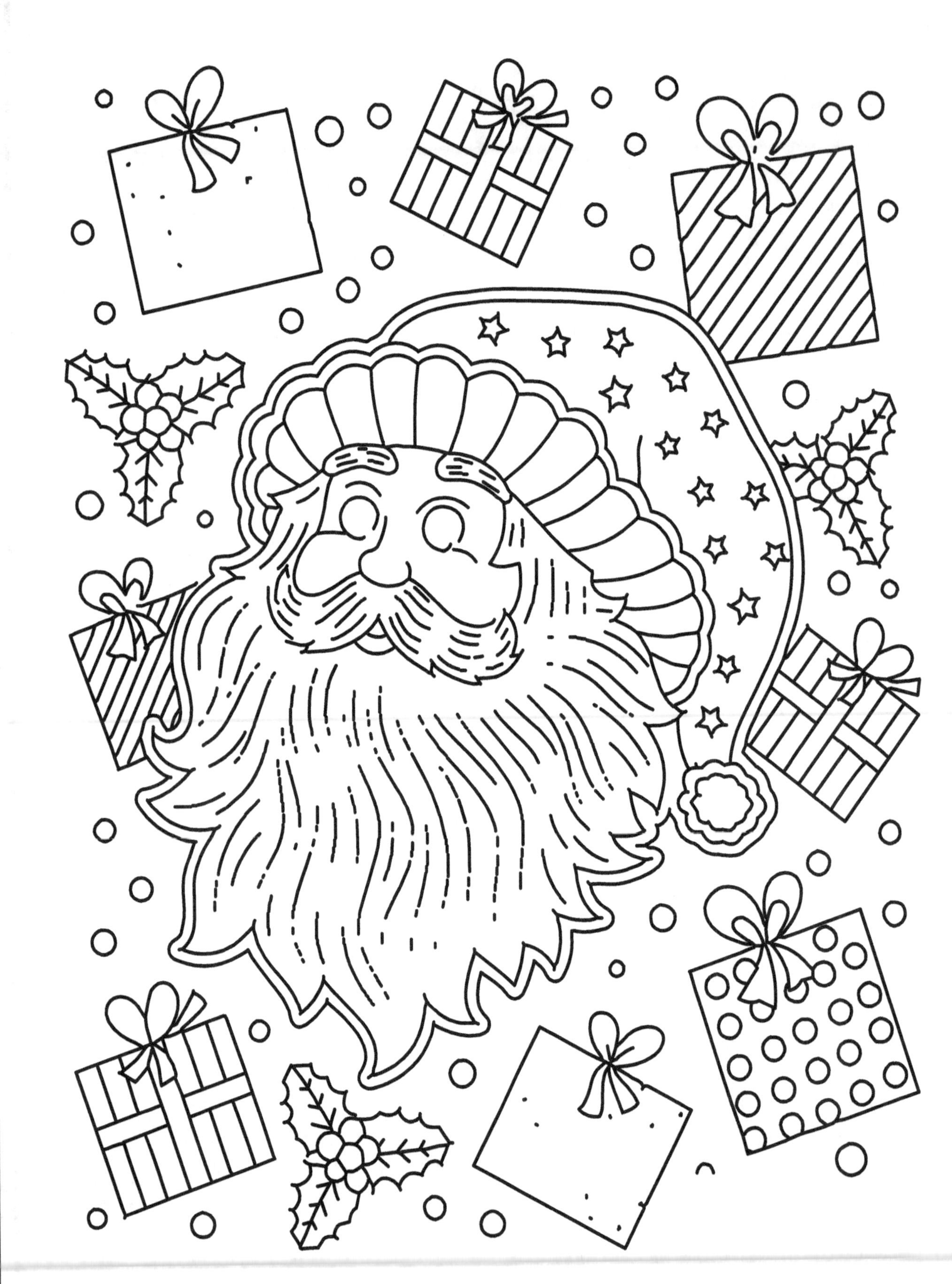

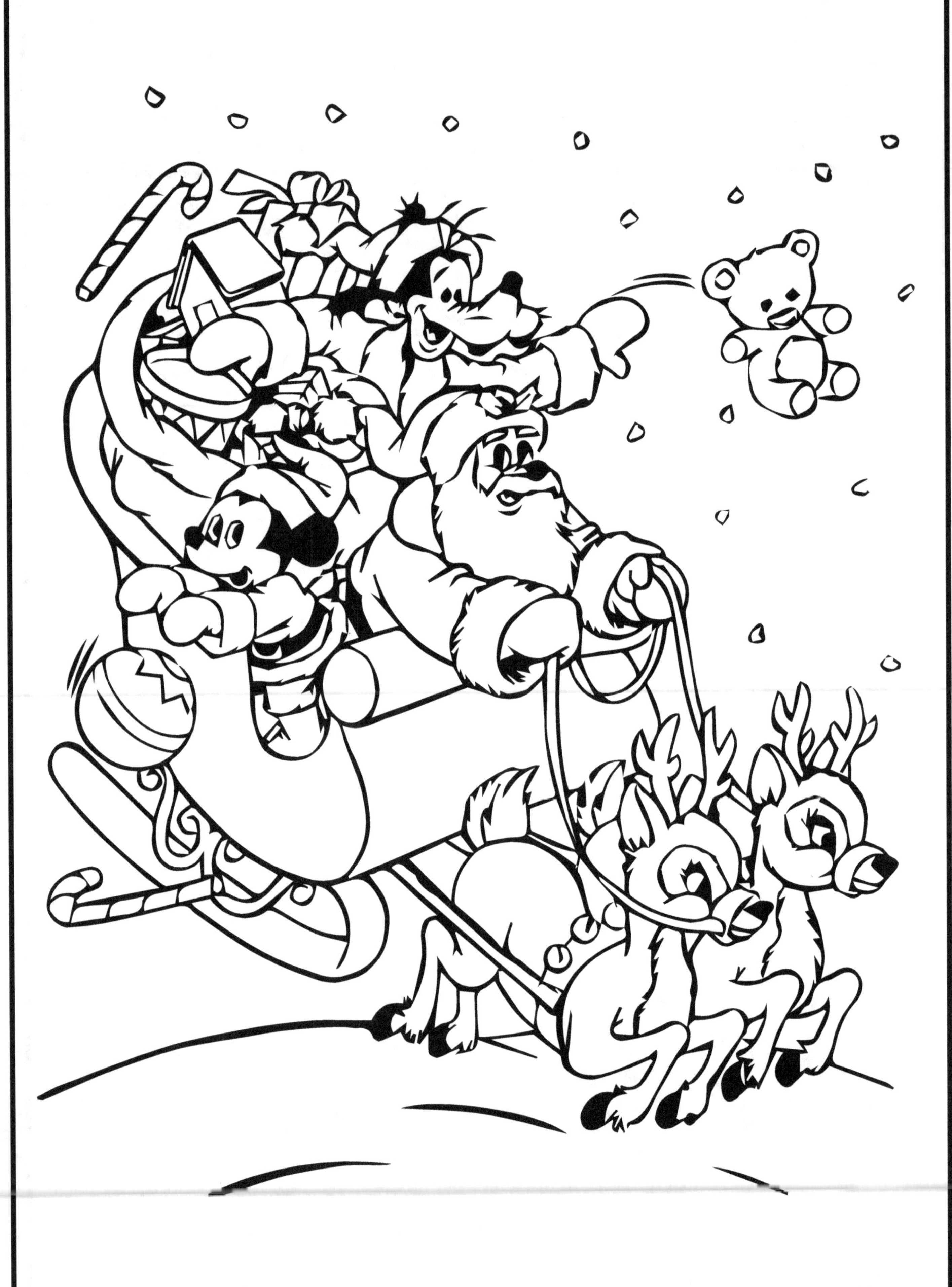

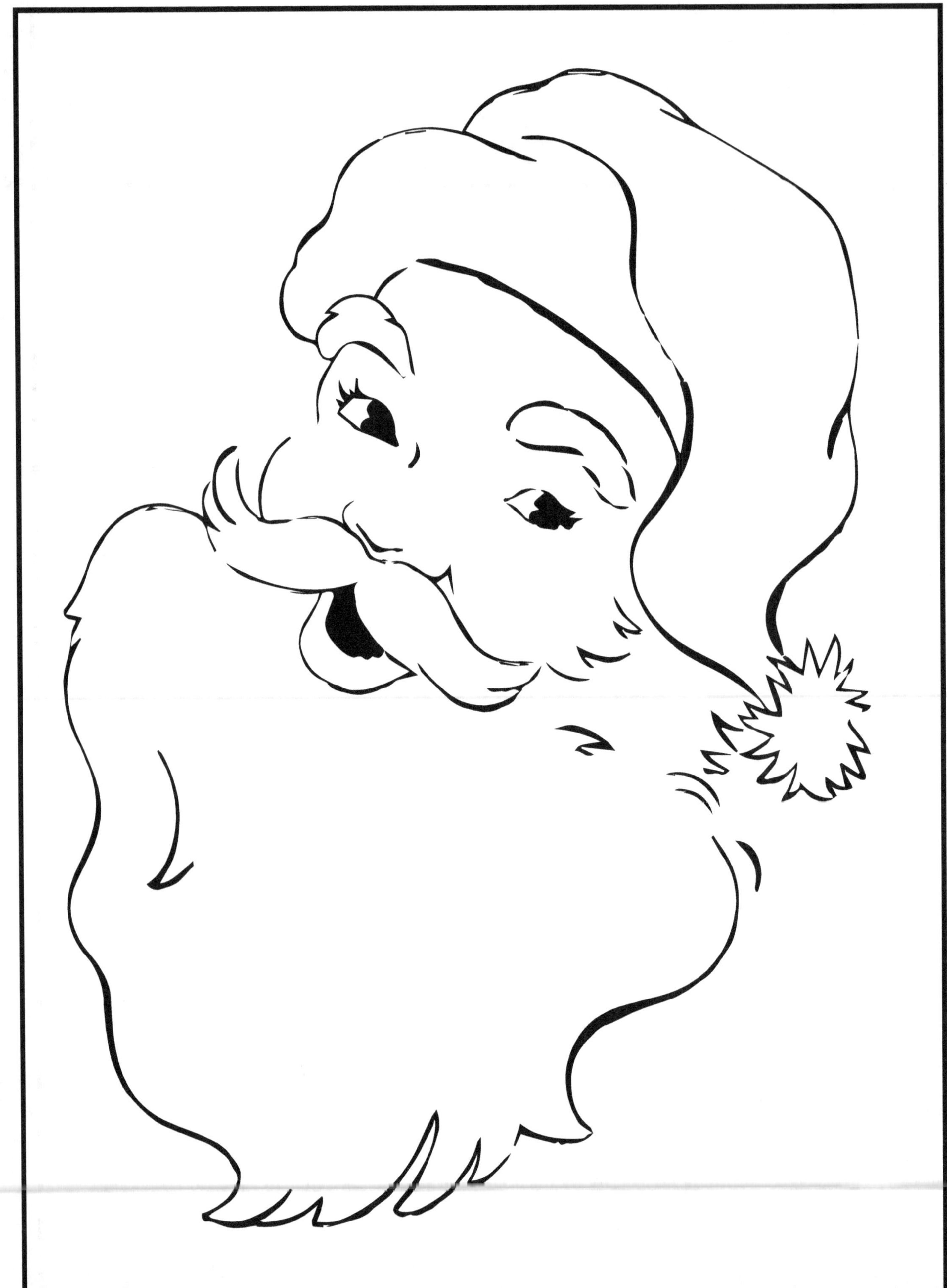